THE INSIDE TRACK

THE INSIDE TRACK

Paddocks, Pit Stops and Tales of Life in the Fast Lane

JAKE HUMPHREY

**SIMON &
SCHUSTER**

London · New York · Sydney · Toronto · New Delhi

A CBS COMPANY

For Steve Vickerstaff and Gemma Barrett, who are both sadly missed but act as a daily reminder to savour every moment

First published in Great Britain by Simon & Schuster UK Ltd, 2012
A CBS COMPANY

Simon & Schuster UK Ltd
1st Floor
222 Gray's Inn Road
London
WC1X 8HB

www.simonandschuster.co.uk

Simon & Schuster Australia, Sydney
Simon & Schuster India, New Delhi

A CIP catalogue record for this book is available from the British Library

HB ISBN: 978-1-84983-724-8
TPB ISBN: 978-1-84983-725-5
eBook ISBN: 978-1-84983-727-9

Typeset by Hewer Text UK Ltd, Edinburgh
Printed and bound in Great Britain by CPI Group (UK) Ltd, Croydon, CR0 4YY

Contents

The warm-up

Sometimes in my job the drama doesn't only unfold on the track. On occasions we've had all of our technical equipment fail just minutes before the live programme. That is an unbelievably nerve-wracking experience. Suddenly everything – planned guests, locations and talking points – goes out of the window. That's when we head to what we call the 'bolt hole'.

All our technical equipment operates using radio waves, but as a back-up we have an area we can go where everything gets plugged in with wires. It's safe, reliable, but pretty restricting. I'll never forget the time, standing in the pit lane in Hockenheim for the German Grand Prix, when all of a sudden my earpieces went silent. We were minutes from going live; cue frantic looks among the team as we quickly established that everyone had lost all form of communication. In the pit lane we were totally helpless. As we raced to the bolt hole, my mind turned to how we might fill an hour's build-up if we couldn't move anywhere. I concentrated on trying to stay as calm as possible. Ideally the viewers at home would remain unaware of any problem at all – and that's when you earn your money.

Moments like that I compare to a swan paddling frantically against the current under the water, while all you see above the surface is a serene, calm vision of confidence. At least, that's the idea.

There are many variables in this job. A pit lane that resembles Times Square while an engine roars up behind you; trying to guide two experts while looking out for a guest; knowing what the next link is, and then stopping to the second it's all over.

And the greatest thrill of all for me? That we broadcast live from the paddock and pit lane, not from a comfy, warm studio. I struggle to think of a place less well suited to easy television than a pit lane but, boy, it certainly makes for dramatic viewing.

The few hundred fans in there with us before the race are the fortunate ones. With tens of millions tuning into the drama on TV sets around the world, these lucky men, women and children are actually spitting distance from an F1 car and the hallowed, spotless hives of activity that are the teams' garages. Even more than that, in an hour this pit lane will be the focus of the race. Some will be the guests of sponsors, others competition winners, or perhaps they simply know the people to know! Most will have paid a whopping premium to stand in there, in the midday sun, and smell the oil, hear the engines, feel the energy.

And it was against this backdrop that we went live to the nation in Melbourne in March 2009. With all that going on around you it's so easy to get carried away and speak too fast, try and cram too much into a sentence or transmit everything you can see and feel to the viewer. At that moment, however, I was in survival mode – just get through this first broadcast and all will be okay. I hoped.

How I became an F1 presenter

In the autumn of 2008, I was scooped up from the friendly, colourful, smiley world of children's television and pitched headfirst into one of the most high-profile, ruthless and exciting sports on the planet: Formula One. I'm often told, via Twitter, blogs and sometimes straight to my face as I walk down the street, that I must have 'one of the best jobs in the world', and I would never argue with that. I get the chance to travel the world, watch sporting history being made, meet global icons and deal with the cut and thrust of live television on a weekly basis.

Of course, a whole lot more goes on behind the scenes of Formula One than the glamorous bits, and with every job come challenges, but no matter the highs and the lows, I always carry with me the saying we use in my family: 'Roots and wings'. For me, the phrase is a constant reminder of the importance of a strong, stable, supportive home life. To use the latter, you need to have the former; roots provide you with a solid and stable background that gives you the confidence to use your wings. Great wings that carry us across oceans are wonderful, but without firm roots we wouldn't have the courage to use them, and eventually we'd come crashing down. Up until the age of twenty-eight, I hadn't really needed to use my wings at all, and I probably wasn't aware just how strong my roots were. Then, on 3 September 2008, I was offered the chance to present the BBC's Formula One coverage, and I've hardly stopped beating my wings since.

Following in the footsteps of the consummate professional Steve Rider, and the dedicated ITV Sport team behind him, was always going to be a daunting task, and let's just say that my first production meeting at the BBC didn't exactly get off to a flying start. It was the first time we'd all be together in the same room – not only would the programme-makers be present, but also my new on-screen family: Martin Brundle, who is without doubt one of the greatest F1 commentators we've had in this country; Eddie Jordan, who used to fill my living room with a burst of vibrant yellow every weekend when I watched the Grands Prix as a kid; and finally David Coulthard, who was a star of British motorsport for well over a decade. These were people I had watched and admired for years, and suddenly here I was, required not only to be their colleague, but also to strike up an instant rapport with them. Not the most natural of things, I can assure you.

An initial hello was going to be nerve-wracking enough,

and I was keen to get off to a good start when we all met up. Unfortunately, the reality of what happened couldn't have been further from what I'd planned! Our meeting was scheduled for 10am at west London's BBC Television Centre, and I was running late. My family and friends will testify that this is pretty normal for me, but I'd hoped that with light traffic and a little bit of luck, it might just be all right. It wasn't. You know one of those journeys where at every turn you take you're faced with brake lights? When, as soon as you do a U-turn out of a traffic jam, the cars start moving again? Well, that was my morning and, as I sat in the car, panic rising up through my body, all hopes of getting off on the right foot were blown. I was 20 minutes late. To make matters worse, the meeting was in a boardroom on the sixth floor – a large, quiet, echoing room at the best of times. I arrived, peered through the crack in the door and saw twenty or so people gathered around an oval table – the meeting had clearly started without me.

Suffice it to say, it's difficult to sneak unnoticed into a room when you're six foot three and the door ccrrreeeaaakkkkks open to announce your arrival. No one really knew me at all at that point and, as every single face turned to look at me, it's fair to say that first impressions weren't good. And this was before I had grasped exactly how important it is to stick religiously to schedules and timings in F1. I slid into the glaringly vacant seat and squeaked, 'There was an accident!' The boss leant in towards me and said, 'There will be.' I consoled myself with the thought that things could only get better from there . . .

I have always loved F1, perhaps because I'm a Norfolk boy and my home county has a long and distinguished history of motor racing. Nigel Mansell drove the famous black and gold Lotus, Ayrton Senna lived in Norwich as a young guy, and people there have a real passion for grass-roots motorsport: stock car racing, speedway, club races at Snetterton on a windy Norfolk afternoon – most of the county is motor racing mad. Throw into the mix my Uncle Michael's racing success, and I guess that is where it all started for me. My uncle was a local super stock racer of some repute, but to an impressionable 7-year-old he was my very own Stirling Moss.

So when, in early 2008, I heard that the BBC had secured the rights to Formula One, you can imagine how excited I felt. It was a big commitment for a publicly funded channel – figures in their tens of millions were being bandied about as the price of obtaining the contract – and the pressure for the programme to be a success was huge. The papers were full of speculation: would the famous 'The Chain' theme tune return? Would Murray Walker be back in the commentary box? Would Martin Brundle jump ship from ITV? And the most thrilling question of all – who would the new presenter be?

At this time, I was still presenting at Children's BBC, merrily carrying on the baton from John Craven as the host of *Newsround*, but I was also starting to dip my toe into the warm waters of BBC Sport. Live sports programming had been my real aim ever since I started as a television runner in the 1990s so, as I read reports in the papers that Richard Hammond, Gabby Logan, Chris Evans and Jeremy Clarkson were all in the running to take on the F1 role, I made a pact with myself. I felt it would be a little arrogant to chase the F1 job and expect it to drop into my lap, but I also knew it was my dream role. So I decided the right approach was to make it abundantly clear that I'd love the job, but only to do that if it was mentioned to me.

The year progressed, and having convinced the BBC Sport department to take a chance on a children's TV presenter and let me do a couple of stints here and there, hosting *Football Focus* and doing some sports reporting, I was given the opportunity to broadcast from the European Football Championship. It was at the Euros that the words 'Formula' and 'One' were first mooted to me. I was asked if I liked the sport and whether I knew much about it, to which I responded positively. Nothing more was said for a few weeks and I thought my chance had gone. Meanwhile, almost every time I picked up the paper it felt as if another name was being linked with the job. Strangely, no one ever mentioned the guy who had hosted such shows as *Rule the School*, *Bamzooki* and *Gimme a Break*, while also dressing up as a pink shellfish and running around the *Blue Peter* garden popping foam-filled balloons for 'Mobster Lobster'.

Following the Euros, I hosted my first Olympics, in Beijing

in August 2008, and while I was there I met with the Head of Sport at the BBC, who would very much be part of the F1 decision. We touched on the subject, but he certainly gave nothing away. If they were considering me, they were playing a great game of poker. A couple of days after I got back from China, I was asked to submit a document detailing how I'd host F1 if I got the chance. A few days after that, I went to a meeting at BBC Television Centre, where I chatted with the department bosses about the new F1 contract and the opportunities it might present me. Then, strangely, they asked me to count the steps from the office to the lift and then come back into the room. I will never forget what they said when I went back in: 'Mr Sloane [Niall, then BBC Head of Football and Motor Racing] and Mr Wilkin [Mark, the current editor of the programme] would like to offer you the job as our new F1 presenter.' My reply? 'Mr Humphrey would be delighted to accept!'

I could have exploded. All my Christmases, birthdays and Easters came at once in that moment. Needless to say, I immediately broke the rules of confidentiality and cried down the phone to my mum and dad. I was asked to keep it a secret until one Thursday in a few weeks' time, when they'd announce the news. In the meantime, I had to bite my lip and keep schtum. Not easy for me. I also spent the intervening weeks wondering when they'd either ring me up and say, 'Only joking!', or realise they'd made a huge mistake and retract the offer. It was a nail-biting time. Roll forward to the day of the announcement about the new BBC F1 team and 20 minutes after the news broke, my phone rang. It was my wife. 'I've just been on the internet,' she sobbed, 'and everyone thinks you're going to be rubbish!' Now, I wasn't used to being recognised in my own house, so you can imagine what a shock this scrutiny came as. I told her not to worry and asked where she'd read it. 'On the BBC website,' she said. Oh dear.

Suddenly, not only did I have to prepare myself for the most demanding live TV you can imagine, show Eddie Jordan and David Coulthard that I was up to the job and make sure I didn't let the production down, but now I also had to prove that the naysayers were wrong and that the doubters had judged me too quickly. There was only one way through this and it involved doing my prep, trusting my instincts and hoping people liked the 'new-look' F1 team.

Early on in my career, I received a sage piece of advice from one of my old bosses – 'Never sit in the comfy chair' – and I like to think I've taken those words on board. This job isn't particularly comfy, that's for sure! Not only are you away from your home and your family for a good part of the year, but most days you are outside for about six or seven hours, whether that's in searing heat, a mild breeze or torrential rain. You don't have the benefit of rehearsals; there's no make-up, no autocue to tell you what you're going to say next. Quite often there isn't even the luxury of a running order. In the post-race segment especially, we really are just busking it, and reacting to whatever drama live television has thrown our way.

Take Canada 2011 as a prime example. We were midway through a season that had been dominated by Sebastian Vettel. Every time you walked into the paddock, you saw the crush of reporters gathered outside his team HQ, or witnessed him having to sprint from the hospitality suite to the back of the garage just to avoid the autograph hunters and journalists desperate for a story. The weekend had progressed like any other; just as he had done for the previous few races, Vettel had shown incredible bravery and raw speed to stick his car on pole position. I was in the paddock that evening, listening to the drivers and chatting to the team bosses as they resigned themselves to the fact that Sebastian was going to pull his usual trick – he has an impressive ability to get the perfect start, which is not easy when you have to keep the revs at the precise bite point, release not one but two clutches on the rear of the steering wheel and get the right amount of drive off the line without getting so much that you spin the rear wheels. Once you've started moving, you then have to hit the KERS (Kinetic Energy Recovery System) button for an extra boost of power as soon as you're going over 100kph, change up through the gears while keeping your eye on the first turn, all the time making sure you defend your position from over twenty cars flying along behind you at speeds of up to 200mph. Seb managed to do this race after race, keeping hold of the lead while increasing the gap between himself and the rest of the drivers, so giving that little bit of breathing space. He was starting to look unbeatable, uncatchable.

But not on this occasion, not as the rains came.

'How can they be the best drivers in the world if they can't cope with rain?' some people scoff. An F1 car works on the principle of downforce, and to 'switch on' that ability to stick to the road you need to be going at a certain speed. Added to that, you need heat in the tyres before they become grippy and stick to the track, and the brakes have to be red-hot before they will stop the car sufficiently. In the rain, not only is it hard for the drivers to employ downforce and heat as effectively, but there is also another issue to consider: an F1 car runs so close to the ground that the 'plank' underneath is just a few millimetres off the floor. In wet weather, too much water on the track turns the plank into a canoe, and the car is washed clean off the asphalt and on to the grass or into the gravel. And all this is before you take into account the lack of visibility.

So there we were in Canada, with drivers telling their teams the rain is too heavy and cars slipping off all over the place; our broadcasting team was huddled in various garages, in an attempt to find shelter at a track that has hardly changed since the 1960s, where the hospitality units are tiny and temporary and the TV compound is a long walk away. The crowds may have been soaked but they were also mesmerised as Jenson Button crashed with his teammate Lewis Hamilton (resulting in Hamilton's retirement), got a puncture, tangled with

Fernando Alonso, made pit stop after pit stop and at one point was running last. At this stage, Seb had hardly put a foot wrong; despite his tender years and massive inexperience compared to Jenson, it was almost inconceivable that he'd give in to the pressure he was under. After all, he was the world champion. And then F1 did what it does best – it delivered a story that even George Lucas, who was at the race, would have struggled to imagine. While his rivals were on the slower, wet-weather tyres, Jenson fitted slick tyres, overtook rival cars as if they were standing still and on the final lap suddenly he had Vettel in his sights.

I was sitting, soaked to the core, just ten feet from Lewis Hamilton, who had long since made his way to the team hospitality unit. The room was electric as Jenson honed in on Sebastian. Jenson's family and friends were in a group, huddled around one television; the catering staff and guests, including the pop star Rihanna, were watching the final few minutes of a race that had lasted over four hours. I was actually head down, making notes for the end of the programme, when I heard a loud gasp. Lewis sat bolt upright and everyone turned to the screen. Sebastian had slid to the right around a left-handed corner, the result of having let his car run wide on to the wet part of the track, and Jenson slithered by like the wind. Just a few corners later and the win was his. The emotion was unbridled – the motorhome erupted, and it was great to see Lewis clapping his teammate as Jenson Button picked up the most dramatic victory of his career.

To sum up a race like that for the audience at home, you need to rely on all your experience but most importantly you have to trust your instinct. In situations like these, there is simply no time to plan what we're going to say, the areas of the race we'll analyse or how we'll sign off the programme. And that is exactly why live sport is such a thrilling challenge for a presenter.

Rewind to my first ever broadcast, remove some of the familiarity that three seasons' worth of experience brings, and the first time we went live was terrifying. But during that first transmission also came one of my proudest moments: when we were midway through the build-up to the first qualifying session, Martin Brundle joined us live and said he thought we – David Coulthard, Eddie Jordan and myself – looked like we'd been working together forever. And, to be honest, that is how it felt from the very beginning. I think we all contribute to the presenting team in our own ways; DC and EJ bring their knowledge and experience of the sport, and I hope I bring my experience of presenting and my enthusiasm for F1.

Luckily for me, Formula One is a sport that's easy to get enthusiastic about. I've witnessed some great moments of sporting triumph, and I've seen some terrifying collisions. I've interviewed drivers as they celebrate their victories and as they battle with their disappointments. I've experienced moments in my career when I wished the ground would swallow me up, and I've stood on tracks where history has been made and lives have been lost. Of course, there's the obvious thrill of the fast cars, the death-defying race tracks, the glamorous settings, the determination and the devotion of the drivers and their teams. But this sport is about so much more than speed and bravery – it's an incredible engineering battle as well. So much of what happens out on the track is a direct result of what takes place behind the closed doors of team headquarters. To really understand the sport, you need to realise that the biggest battle of all is the development race. While the teams are fighting to win the title they are at the same time already focusing manpower, effort and energy on the following season.

Once you've built and improved the car to a sufficient level it then becomes about teamwork. Not only in the racing, but in the mammoth logistical challenge of travelling the world, constantly feeding back to an army of workers at the team's base as the race weekend progresses. The unseen race is just as astounding and inspiring as what unfolds on the track. And the reason for it all? Man's natural desire to compete and to win, but not at all costs. Until you've stepped inside it, it's impossible to appreciate just how close the F1 family is, how the drivers, engineers, team principals and journalists all exist within a 'bubble' of travelling, working, failing and succeeding together. And when they need to, they are all there to support each other – from Felipe Massa's accident that almost cost him his life to the remarkable way the pit lane came together as one when fire ripped through the Williams garage just hours after one of their greatest triumphs.

F1 is a global adventure that is a true World Championship. It covers every corner of the globe, arouses every human emotion, and provides drama and intrigue that has millions glued to their television sets for the whole season. And the most compelling part of the sport? That we witness the greatest collection of drivers in the world going wheel-to-wheel every other week; and whether they succeed or fail, they return the following week to try again. The sport doesn't dwell on defeat, victory doesn't make it rest on its laurels. It's the sport that never takes its foot off the pedal, and whether you're driving the car, making decisions from the pit wall, cheering in the stands or glued to the TV, there is something for everyone.

1

In at the deep end

The day of my first F1 broadcast for the BBC – 28 March 2009 – was the most scared, lonely and inferior I have felt in my entire life. It might seem strange that a feeling of inferiority was my overriding emotion; after all, I had been chosen to front the return of Formula One to the BBC after a thirteen-year absence, and I've been on the TV since the age of eighteen. You see, the mistake I had made was to attend the Chinese Grand Prix a few months before.

As much as my family enjoyed motorsport during my formative years in Norfolk, we never really had the money to attend Grands Prix when I was a kid. So when I was given the F1 job the BBC wisely thought it best not to make my first race the opening Grand Prix of 2009, which I would be presenting live to the nation! Therefore, in late October 2008 I went to China to meet David Coulthard, who was racing in his final season before retirement, and to watch my first ever live Formula One Grand Prix.

The funny thing about being a TV presenter is that there are no qualifications to do the job – no degree certificate that says people will like you, no courses you can attend to be natural and likable when in front of the camera. It's incredibly subjective, which means one person may love what you do and another simply can't stand you. Doing this job, you have to block these thoughts out and trust your instincts. You also need a pretty thick skin and a smattering of confidence; after all, you have to believe people are going to want to hear what you have to say. There is simply no hiding place. I will never forget the moment that confidence deserted me entirely and I was hit by the dawning realisation that I wasn't going to be able to do the job: I was in way over my head, entirely out of my depth, and the whole thing was going be a career-ending disaster.

I had been feeling relaxed and confident as the director and the editor of the new show and I meandered around the Shanghai paddock and team homes, introducing ourselves to people and explaining that we were soon to take over the TV coverage. The paddock in China is vast, built just after the millennium when China was keen to do things quicker, bigger, higher than anywhere else. Therefore, in Shanghai the grandstand is about half a mile long and stretches up to the heavens, while they also constructed what was at the time the longest straight in F1 – just because they could! The first thing that struck me about the world of F1 as we walked around was the strong sense of being a community. Even then, not knowing anyone in the paddock, I started to see how things worked, and I stood and observed for a while. There was a lot to absorb and many new faces to get to know, but that warm, overcast October afternoon was great. I felt good.

But as a chillier, more autumnal wind began whistling through the circuit and kicking up the dust, as engines roared in the distance and the now familiar whiff of fuel and oil filled my nostrils for the first time, my good spirits began to evaporate. My general mood of excitement and impatience suddenly began to give way to a strange feeling of loneliness – it was as if I had been pitched into a party where everyone knew each other except me. I watched the cameramen as they seemed instinctively to know where to wait to get the right photos and video footage of the drivers, while the journalists moved around in a hunting pack, going from team home to team home at set times to get the drivers' thoughts. Mechanics high-fived each other as they walked to and from the garage, while outside each garage stood large, stern-looking security guards stopping any unwanted guests. It was clear that there was a set of rules that had to be obeyed and that the people here already knew the protocol inside out; the expectations, and the boundaries. I understood then that it was going to be a steep learning curve, but I tried not to let things overwhelm me – after all, I told myself, I wasn't going to be able to understand every last detail of the sport and be accepted all on my first day, was I?

The following morning we returned for qualifying, and I met David Coulthard for the first time. He was standing at the back of the garage, much thinner than he seemed on TV, with greying hair and the really assured ease of a man completely at home. Zipping up his race suit and chatting to his race engineer, he was every inch the racing star. All drivers have a race engineer, and they need an almost telepathic relationship with them, and to trust them completely. While the driver wrestles a multimillion-pound, precious and easily broken prototype of a car around the track at hundreds of miles an hour, the race engineer's job is to explain the strategy decisions the team are making, describe the race situation as succinctly as possible, and keep his driver calm or fire him up when needed.

David eventually finished his chat with his engineer, 'Rocky' – who now engineers Sebastian Vettel – and invited us to put on headphones and listen in to his team attack qualifying. Wow! It may seem an odd analogy, but I would liken the experience to the first time I went snorkelling on holiday – suddenly you have access to a world that you didn't even know existed. David and the team went through radio checks and then discussed when they would head out for qualifying, how many laps they'd do and the tyres they'd use. Suddenly the jovial, welcoming garage grew very loud and incredibly serious, and I tried to make myself as inconspicuous as possible at the back. Not that easy when you are as tall as I am!

It was a real education as David went out, set a hot lap and then pulled back into the pits. Even then, at the back of the garage and with noise-cancelling headphones on, I was blown away by the aggression and the ferocity of the cars – the wheel-spinning and laying down rubber as the car shot out of the pit box, the dust and fumes it kicked up on its return, and the searing heat from the engine, exhaust, brakes and tyres. Everything was far more heightened than it had ever appeared on the television. I could just see the rear wing of the cars over the pit wall as they shot down the main straight. 'That can't be how fast they actually are,' I thought as they shot by at 200mph, a breathtaking wall of noise. David's session was actually impeded by Nick Heidfeld, who was driving for BMW Sauber, and as he got out of the car you could tell by his body language that things hadn't gone as planned. F1 is a high-stakes, high-pressure and big-money game. At that moment I kept my distance.

If that morning was unnerving, it was nothing compared to what I experienced the next afternoon. It was race day, 30 minutes before the start, and I couldn't believe how alive everything felt. There is a real change in the energy at a Formula One event with half an hour to go until lights out. When you consider that there are only twenty races annually – as many races in one year as there are Premier League football matches in just one fortnight – you realise why mistakes are rarely tolerated. Everyone is expected to match up to the highest standards – suddenly everything is urgent, serious and completely controlled.

Standing in the Red Bull garage, having wished a focused David Coulthard the best of luck, I noticed ITV's Steve Rider, who was just a few feet away in the pit lane. He was the man I would be replacing, and he was standing with Mark Blundell – his pundit – and four crew members. That was it. Six people, alone, in a vast pit lane. There were mechanics rushing nearby, cars screaming past at 60mph on their way to the grid, other cars burning off fuel by driving through the pit lane, equipment being transported, camera crews and journalists everywhere, a vast grandstand full of tens of thousands of people – and then the ITV crew, so small, so insignificant and so alone, looking incredibly vulnerable.

The TV compound, where the other members of the production team sit, can be a mile away from the pit lane where the broadcast happens and there are no cables, there is no physical, tangible connection to the rest of the team. Just a microphone, an earpiece and gallons of trust. Trust that you will deliver, that the team will help you out if you need it, and that the technical side of the operation will cope with the rigours of live F1. You really do have to pin your hopes on all these things happening, because on the other side of that camera are a few million people. No autocue, no scriptwriters, no rehearsals, no delayed transmission, no safety net. Fall, or even wobble, and it's likely to be game over – and a very public game over at that.

It was at precisely this moment that I was struck by the enormity of it all; and it felt as if my world had come crashing down around me. Suddenly I longed for the comfort of introducing *Tracy Beaker* or *Blue Peter* in the safe, multicoloured world of the CBBC channel. The boss looked at me and said, 'What are you thinking?'

'Exciting,' I said. 'Can't wait 'til it's us.'

I was lying.

I had just about managed to compose myself by the time David brought the car home in tenth place, and Lewis Hamilton had won the race in emphatic style just weeks before he was crowned world champion in dramatic fashion in Brazil, where he overtook a car on the final corner of the final lap of the final race that year to bag the title.

Five months later, and I had swapped smoggy China for sunny Melbourne. Well over 100,000 people were packed into Albert Park, in the middle of this vibrant, modern Australian city, and now it was my turn. Fleetwood Mac's 'The Chain' is blasting down my earpiece, the PA says 'Twenty seconds left on VT', I've written my script and I know that my mum and dad, my wife, my bosses, my peers and colleagues, and millions of viewers, are about to make up their minds about whether I am the man for the job.

That first walk into the pit lane was a real eye-opener. Most pit lanes are about fifteen feet wide, which is no problem once the cars are on track and the pit lane is limited to just essential team personnel, but 60 minutes pre-race it's a rather different story. The pit lane is the heartbeat of an F1 track, so for a few hundred – and sometimes thousand – pounds sterling, a lucky few can pay to see and be seen above and around the teams' garages during a race. And as I walked into the pit lane for the first time, it felt like the whole of Melbourne was in there: a wall of bodies, all resplendent in Ferrari hats, McLaren tops or Red Bull jackets – it was a bit like walking on to a packed platform on the London Underground in rush hour, but in Technicolor. People were taking photos, pushing and elbowing for the best view of the cars, while barriers and security personnel stopped them from getting close enough to prevent the team from doing their work. Amid all this mayhem, I was going to try and present a live TV show – and so began the learning curve.

It's incredible, looking back now, to think just how little I really knew about the business of getting the cars on track back in 2009. I recall, at my first race, the producer telling me, 'The pit lane is now open, so be careful,' and thinking, 'What is he talking about?' What he meant was that, with 30 minutes to go until the start of the race, it was time for the cars to make it round to the grid – it sounded simple enough but, as I was soon to find out, in F1 nothing is simple. At about 20 minutes past the hour, I noticed all the mechanics streaming out of the garages like little uniformed ants, each representing their chosen team. They lined up by a gate to the track, waiting to be allowed on to the grid – everything is timed and calculated to the minute, and everyone knows that breaking the rules can lead to a severe punishment. With these mechanics and engineers was an unbelievable amount of kit. Unlike your or my road car, you can't just turn off an F1 car and leave it, then return to it, turn the key and expect it to start up. These cars are effectively alive, and they need a full 'life-support' system to keep them happy until the start of the race. The engineers were also taking laptops on to the grid in order to capture thousands of bits of data from the cars every minute; they had spare tyres in case the weather changed, tyre warmers to make sure the tyres weren't cold and therefore offering too little grip; a starter gun because the driver doesn't start the car himself; four wheel guns to get the wheels on and off, not to mention umbrellas, trolleys of extra kit, and those important little things like drinks for the driver – essential because of the fluid lost during a race. Once the equipment was on the grid and laid out at each of the starting positions, the engineers waited for the cars to leave their respective garages. Precisely 30 minutes before the race start, the pit lane light went green, the V8 engines sprang to life, and you needed eyes in the back of your head to make sure you didn't get hit. No mean feat when you're concentrating on the job in hand and also wearing ear defenders to avoid being deafened by the sound of the cars.

I'm pleased to say that I survived the madness of my first pit lane in Melbourne in 2009. The race was a great return of

Formula One to the BBC, and also marked a fantastic change in fortunes for Jenson Button, following Honda's shock with-drawal from F1 in December 2008. Just months before the new season, I received a phone call from a producer at work, saying, 'Only one British driver for the new F1 season, hey?' It was news to me, and when I went online I saw that Honda had pulled the plug, leaving Jenson Button without a drive for 2009 and Lewis Hamilton as the sole British representative on the grid.

To say that this was an unexpected turn of events was an understatement. Just a few days before, I had spent the after-noon being introduced to the press officers at the Honda HQ, who operated out of an unassuming building in Brackley, just off the A43 in Northamptonshire. We were fed sandwiches in the boardroom and taken to the silent design office. It was full of people designing new front wings, exhaust systems and trick diffusers; they tapped away on their PCs, the latest design software on the screen in front of them, as they used their know-how to develop something they thought would make all the difference come the start of the season. All the talk was of the team's hopes for the future, and indeed the purpose of our tour was to discuss how we would work with them in the coming season.

In many ways, the fate of Honda was a perfect first lesson in how Formula One works. It's a ruthless, transient world where the clock and the balance sheet judge you. Unfortunately for Honda, neither stacked up in their favour. Despite the tens of millions they were pumping into their F1 bid, the previous season had yielded just fourteen points and a ninth-place finish out of the eleven teams. It wasn't good enough, and the decision was taken in Japan to simply pull the plug and get out now.

Sadly for the Japanese employees who returned home, they had designed a car that they would never see race under the Honda flag. Many feared it would be stillborn, but after plenty of high-level discussions it was decided that Ross Brawn, the multitalented, multi-title-winning former Ferrari designer would perform a management takeover with his investors and partners. Little was he to know that taking the reins would be one of the greatest decisions of his career.

If pre-season testing was impressive, that first race in Melbourne was just unreal. Brawn GP, as they were now known, had a white car almost completely devoid of sponsors' logos. A few years before, you couldn't move for companies clamouring to advertise on an F1 car, but pretty much the only sponsorship this car displayed was that of Richard Branson's Virgin Group. It was a stark reminder that in 2009 the financial world was starting to implode, and convincing companies to part with their cash to sponsor an F1 car that hadn't even been due to race just a few weeks before was clearly a difficult sell. It must have been a dream for Richard Branson, though – his Virgin logo took pride of place on the side of the cockpit, and a predominantly white car with little flashes of fluorescent yellow took to the track while Sir Richard prowled around in the paddock.

And when the car did race, what a machine it proved to be. Remarkably, this team, who were only there by the skin of their teeth, were fastest in Saturday's qualifying session, and by some margin. On that day the top ten on the grid were split by just one second, yet six-tenths of a second separated Jenson Button in first and Sebastian Vettel in third. Okay, just over half a second is the blink of an eye, but in F1 that's a lifetime, as often just hundredths of a second can separate teams on the grid after racing each other over three miles. We knew the car was rumoured to be quick, but it hadn't topped the time sheets all weekend in practice. As I watched the drama unfold on a TV screen in the paddock, I turned to the producer alongside me and we both broke into a huge grin. This was going to be some story to cover.

So, Jenson Button took pole position with teammate Rubens Barrichello in second; the following day I remember handing to Martin Brundle on the grid, and I'll never forget Jenson's confidence. 'Can you do this?' asked Martin, as he sauntered up to Button, who was standing next to his car. The answer? A simple, resounding, 'Yes.'

And so it proved. Jenson dominated the opening race, and as I made my way out into the pit lane after the chequered flag had gone down, I witnessed something extraordinary: when he drove past as the winner, quite spontaneously the mechanics and engineers from all the teams came out into the pit lane to cheer him home. I've never seen that happen before or since, but Jenson is such a well-liked guy and the Honda situation had sent such shockwaves through the sport that to see him succeed after a setback of that magnitude was a huge relief for everyone involved in F1. Until that point the sport had seemed rather emotionally detached to me, with the focus on figures, downforce and the stopwatch. Not any more. I'm not ashamed to say that watching this impromptu applause made me well up, and that was by no means it for emotion during that first season.

The 2009 season was a real rollercoaster ride for everyone, not least Jenson himself. Getting an insight into the stress an F1 driver has to endure is a part of the job that fascinates me, and this was the first time I really had a chance to see at close quarters the pressure that can build on the shoulders of one guy on a weekly basis. And, boy, did it build on Jenson Button that year! After the first seven races, he had almost double the points of any other driver on the grid. He was sitting pretty on sixty-one points, with his nearest rival – his teammate, Rubens Barrichello – trailing on thirty-five. With ten points available for a win, things were looking rosy for him. As I walked into the paddock with him a couple of races into the season, I could feel the confidence and happiness radiating from him. He was almost bounding towards the motorhome as photographers captured the wide smile on his face, and the prevailing mood at that time was very much one of, 'Just arriving to pick up another victory.'

That's not to say that Button had always been such a dead cert. He arrived in F1 as the next big thing in 2000, at the time making him the youngest ever British driver in the sport, and in his second race he became the youngest ever points-scorer. Certainly he brought with him a level of expectation but, being so young, there had not been too much pressure on him. Then followed some pretty barren years; he finished third in the championship in 2004, but had to wait until 2006 – more than a hundred races into his F1 career – to pick up his first win. So until 2009 he had never before been given the tag of 'favourite' or been expected to win every race and snatch every pole position.

Now, with the birth of Brawn, Jenson's star was on the rise. By the time we got to race eight of the season, the British Grand Prix, people were starting to talk about *when*, not *if* Jenson would be champion . . . and that is when things started to turn. He came home in sixth place at Silverstone, and failed to win the following four races. Suddenly we were in Monza in Italy, and there were only five Grands Prix left to run; the lead he had in the championship was down to just sixteen points, he hadn't scored a podium finish for weeks, and it was my job to find out how he was feeling.

It was a blazing late summer afternoon as I left the TV compound and made my way along the narrow tunnel that runs under the wonderful old Italian Grand Prix circuit in the town of Monza on the outskirts of trendy Milan. The fans were gathering around the entrance to the F1 paddock, hoping to grab a glimpse of their heroes, and, after I'd pushed past the Ferrari backpacks and slid by various large men squeezed into tight-fitting team tops, I entered the paddock and set off to the Brawn GP motorhome for my appointment with Jenson and his press officer. I remember being squashed into a tiny office on the first floor of their rather modest (by F1 standards) motorhome and ludicrously balanced on a beanbag, while we positioned Jenson's chair in front of me and got the cameras into position.

Jenson has never been a difficult interviewee, but on this occasion he looked like a haunted man. He arrived in the room with barely a word for any of us, didn't cut me a second glance as he sat down and, try as I might to get him to open up, his responses were pretty guarded and defensive. This was a man who just wanted to focus on the job behind the wheel, whose dream was slipping away, and here I was quizzing him about it. It's not easy to sit opposite someone and ask why they're struggling at their job, particularly when that person knows that what they say will be shared with millions. It's a rather false environment and one that isn't conducive to complete frankness; in a sport such as F1, particularly when your nearest challenger is your teammate, you can't afford to reveal the full truth. Jenson put a brave face on things, but off-camera it was clear to see the strain he was under. Usually, he will chat after an interview, but not on this occasion – his mic was off and he was gone. As I left the motorhome I couldn't help but wonder if his dream of the World Championship was going to be derailed by the pressure on him. If that was how he was in an interview situation, what must the pressure be like as he sat on the grid waiting for the lights to go out and the cars to launch?

Once again, however, this first season was about to take another incredible twist as we headed to Brazil for the penultimate race of the year a few weeks later. The day after our uncomfortable meeting in Italy, Jenson had boosted his chances with a great drive and a podium finish at Monza, and he had carried on picking up points in the run-up to São Paulo. By the time we got to Brazil, and the famous Interlagos circuit, all he needed was a strong finish and the title was his. He arrived with a fourteen-point advantage – if it was ten or more after the race, he was champion.

But to add to the drama of race day, Saturday's qualifying session turned out to be the longest in Formula One history, lasting an astonishing 2 hours 41 minutes thanks to a tropical rainstorm. Imprinted on my memory is the image of myself, David Coulthard and Eddie Jordan huddled under umbrellas, trying to keep out of the rain, while reassuring viewers that we'd soon get action on the track. Contrary to popular belief, neither we nor the teams get any more information than the viewers at home, and we just have to wait for the clouds to clear. At any point the action could start with just a few minutes' warning, which means the teams are constantly having to monitor the weather and work out their strategy – if they get their planning wrong, it can cost them dear. Essentially, the teams have to gamble on when they think the track is going to be at its driest and make sure they are out there, which is a very difficult thing to know. If you've already done lots of laps by the time it gets drier, then you'll have worn out your tyres and won't go quicker; if you don't run the car and the rain continues to get heavier, you've missed the best chance you had to set a quick lap. It's a tricky tactical decision, and one that on this occasion caught Jenson out. There was complete shock in the paddock as he ended up fourteenth on the grid, while his Brazilian teammate Barrichello took pole position at his home event.

That evening I went to the Brawn garage to interview Rubens. As I waited, over walked Jenson, looking mightily relaxed considering the circumstances – a complete contrast to the driver I had interviewed just a few races before. 'How are you feeling?' I asked him. His answer took me aback: 'There's only one way to race this race – chill out with a drink tonight, then tomorrow attack it, have some fun and see how I get on.' He smiled, gave me a wave, and off he wandered.

Twenty-four hours later he did just that: scything through the field, flying past back markers, whooping on the radio as he performed overtakes, and then delivering a bloody awful rendition of Queen's 'We Are The Champions' as he crossed the line. He was a man in his element, and he nailed it that afternoon with the drive of his life, 'the drive of a champion' as David Coulthard described it. Jenson was indeed champion of the world. I've been at World Cup finals (atmosphere like an opera!), Super Bowls (they know how to put on a party in America) and the Olympic Games (always moves me to tears), but nothing has even come close to the raw, honest human emotion I witnessed in Garage 19 in the Interlagos pit lane, Brazil, November 2009.

We had wanted to secure an interview with Jenson if he won the title, but the problem was that Brawn GP hadn't been keen to discuss the matter for fear of jinxing his title charge! After much toing and froing, however, the team promised us they'd do their best to deliver him to us. The late afternoon light was streaming into the garage and, despite the team's win, some of the mechanics were busily trying to pack everything away as they've been trained to, while others discussed their own emotions. Some of Jenson's friends and family were milling around high-fiving people, hugging and sipping on champagne. Then suddenly the attention turned to the latest world champion. With no prior warning and just a few seconds left on a VT we were playing, Jenson appeared, distinctive in his bright white cap and stubble. Wide-eyed and clearly high on a mix of adrenaline, disbelief and sheer joy, he was ushered over to us, followed by an unbelievable flood of people. As we interviewed Jenson, I was being squeezed on all sides by hundreds of photographers jostling to get 'the shot' of the new world champion. I thought at one point we were going to lose Eddie Jordan in the crush, but then my focus switched to the task of delivering an audible first interview worthy of Jenson's achievements. I recently watched it back, and you can see me fighting to keep cameras, microphones and other reporters out of our shot as Jenson plants a kiss on my cheek and tells us how great it feels to fulfil a twenty-year dream.

Despite the hubbub, his emotions were transmitted quite clearly and the mayhem in the garage captured the moment perfectly. During that chat, Jenson mentioned to me that the previous few races had been tough, and as he said those words I was immediately transported back to Monza and that difficult interview in the tiny office. Yet here I was looking at him now and thinking how quickly times of struggle can turn around. In what seemed like the blink of an eye we'd moved from Italy to Brazil and he was now the best in the world. If only he'd known that a few races before, he could have raced much more freely, but that is why sport captures our imagination – we never really know what will happen next.

I remember looking around the room – at the tearful mechanics, the wired photographers, the proud family and team members, my two delighted pundits, Eddie and David, and Jenson at the very centre of it all. He'd driven brilliantly and his place as world champion was secure for eternity. Caught up in the euphoria, along with the heady mix of sweat and champagne, here was a guy clearly still unable to quite deal with the elation of finally realising a dream he'd held dear for over two decades. Formula One drivers are necessarily well trained to thank sponsors and deliver the kind of interviews that won't cause any issues with their fee-paying partners – the cost of F1 is so vast that big-spending and generous sponsors are a must, and what the sponsors get in return for their cash is time on the TV. I am always amazed by the grid walk, when we presenters can bowl up to a driver who is gearing up to race for 90 minutes in sweltering conditions, with both the World Championship and his life on the line, yet he'll still grant us 2 minutes to ask how he's feeling. Can you imagine Manchester United welcoming the cameras into the Old Trafford dressing room just minutes before a Champions League game, reporter in tow? No, me neither! But it felt like fulfilling corporate requirements was at the very back of Jenson's mind at that moment. He was unguarded, emotional, truthful . . . and stunned.

I'll never forget the incredible privilege of sharing those few minutes with him – it's fantastic to see someone's dreams come true, particularly when it's so well deserved. I'll also never forget the letter I received after that interview, from a lady who wrote to tell me that she too was in the garage that day and how wonderful it was to get a better sense than ever before of what it must be like to be crowned a world champion. Just as I was getting to the end of her letter and wondering why she hadn't come over to say hello, she signed off with, 'So thanks for taking me from my living room and dropping me into that garage in Brazil.' That letter has stayed with me ever since, and I regularly think back to it when working out how to deliver a programme or the right thing to say. It felt like quite a journey from that garage in China in 2008 to Brazil just a year later. Just one year, but what a year.

2

The sport that never sleeps

I could barely believe it. Even though the grassy fields all around were wreaking havoc with my hay fever, I was in heaven. I was standing in the building that had helped shape the course of Formula One history: a building that had delivered numerous world champions and had been the scene of both triumph and tragedy over the years. It wasn't glamorous, it wasn't modern, and if it wasn't for the huge yellow badge emblazoned with a black horse rearing up, it would have seemed just like any other business-like collection of industrial-looking units. There was, however, one other tell-tale sign that the square, functional, not-for-show structures were hiding something special. It was their colour. Everywhere was covered in the same deep, familiar hue that immediately conjured up romantic racing images. There was no chrome or glass, no sliding doors or *Star Wars*-style walkways; it was traditional, urbane, not what you'd imagine might get the heart racing, but it did. It was a place every F1 fan would love to visit. It was Ferrari HQ.

On a blazing, bright, late summer's day in Maranello in 2011, I was visiting the oldest, most successful and most evocative Formula One team of them all. I think part of the reason I was so disarmed is that arriving at Ferrari HQ takes you so much by surprise. Maranello itself is a pretty ordinary Italian town just off the A1 motorway, less than an hour from Bologna. You pull off the motorway, on to the Strada Gherbella, left on to the SS12 and eventually you arrive in an Italian town that looks much like so many others – little cafes and trattorias, plenty of Fiats bumbling around as commuters head to work and young mums pushing their kids in prams. Its incredible secret is well hidden until you get closer. In fact, if you didn't know what was there you'd probably think that Modena was the most influential city in the region, famous of course for its balsamic vinegar. But I think Maranello, smaller and just down the road, produces and distributes something far more exciting.

Having arrived and gone through the obligatory security checks we were escorted around the premises by a press officer who clearly reveres the Ferrari name almost as if it were a religion rather than a car maker. The factory does offer a unique experience as the famous road cars are produced and tested in exactly the same place as their F1 cousins. We were taken into a building where young Italian men looked busy and purposeful as they worked away on two F1 chassis, and then it dawned on me where we were – I was standing by the actual F1 race bays. We were in one of the nondescript units, built for function rather than form in the 1940s, while the cars of Felipe Massa and Fernando Alonso were being prepared for the next Grand Prix just feet away from me. At that moment it occurred to me just how few people get to see the secrets behind these hallowed walls. For this reason, F1 fans cannot fully grasp the pressures, the passions and the extreme perfection that resonate through the corridors of the buildings of the F1 teams, driven by one thing – the desire to be the best. Although the various team HQs dotted across Europe might look different from the outside, once you penetrate the mildly paranoid, high-security systems that the teams employ to keep unwanted visitors out, you realise they are essentially all the same.

Running twenty-four hours a day, designing, producing and testing just about every part of an F1 car, from the tiniest nuts and bolts to the vital crash structure that keeps the driver alive, these headquarters are a constant hive of multi-million-pound, high-pressure activity. An F1 car is a complicated jigsaw puzzle made up of 5,000 parts and it's here they design and build those pieces all year long. Housed within these buildings are hundreds of the sharpest and smartest minds the teams can get their hands on – car designers, computer programmers, aerodynamicists, assembly technicians, control system engineers, cooks, truck drivers and cleaners. Each of them is a valued member of the team, and they work in shifts to try to ensure that they are developing at a faster rate than their nearest rivals. It takes up to 500 people and 50,000 man-hours to produce a car considered worthy of taking to the track in Formula One, and it's in these factories, offices and workshops that race-winning cars are born. The result of a team's dedication is a car that changes gear in 10 milliseconds, heats its own tyres to such a degree that you can cook an egg on them, and generates such vicious force under braking that a driver's eyes can sometimes squirt tears on to the inside of his visor. It's enough to make your eyes water!

Formula One operates at the very edge of what is possible. To understand clearly just how on the limit F1 really is, you must consider that small planes can take off at slower speeds than F1 cars travel on the track. For this reason, downforce is king and the quest to find more of it never ceases. When Brawn GP rose from the ashes of the Honda team in 2009, it was downforce that clinched the title for the team and downforce that had cost millions of pounds and thousands of hours to find, the discovery coming in the form of a 'double diffuser'. The diffuser sits low at the rear of the car and is responsible for helping to put the airflow under the car to good use. The Brawn GP car had a controversial hole, which increased the speed of the airflow as it headed towards the higher rear section.

Back in the winter of 2008, even during the uncertain period when Honda announced they were leaving the sport, many in the team would have known that their double diffuser could make a big difference when the cars lined up on the grid for the start of the 2009 season in Melbourne, and they would have been desperate to go racing. You see, no team heads into the first race of the year without a good understanding of how their new car operates; in the months before the start of the season, thousands of bits of information are gathered, either using state-of-the-art computer programmes, 'super-computers' or in a good old-fashioned wind tunnel.

Wind tunnels are so integral to the design process of a car that many teams have traditionally operated theirs twenty-four hours a day, seven days a week, to keep the development rate constant. A wind tunnel can push 9 tonnes of static air over a car at speeds of up to 180kph, and is also crucial in showing how a car will react as it moves through corners. I've heard of F1 cars losing up to 20 per cent of downforce as the car enters a corner, which is exactly the point where you most need the downforce to help you grip the track.

Some of the wind tunnels in F1 can accommodate a full-size car, but most will use much smaller-scale models; as the team adapts the design of even the smallest part of the car, a miniature version will be made for the wind tunnel. If you did design and technology at school, think back to how you'd make a wooden car in your class, spending hours with a plane saw or sanding down a bit of balsa wood before comparing your efforts with those of your mates. That is more or less what they do in F1 – the materials are more state-of-the-art, the precision and attention to detail clearly a little more impressive, but the concept is pretty much the same, and it's quite remarkable to think that that's how an F1 update begins its life.

The wind tunnels themselves can also be super-high-tech; most of those used by F1 teams actually have a 'rolling road' that can run at high speed, allowing teams to simulate a car with rotating tyres. Measuring airflow with rotating wheels is substantially different from measuring airflow with static wheels – again essential to get an accurate reading from the wind tunnel.

Once a car is in the tunnel, updates are constantly added. Some may translate to a big advantage on the track; others may offer improvements worth only hundredths of a second; it's possible that a few updates provide no gain at all. One thing you can be certain of, though: no part will make it to the track until it's been thoroughly checked, tested, double checked and triple tested at the factories. By the time it's produced, each part has delivered thousands of pieces of data to the team and the wind tunnel has even helped work out how the oil in the pipes, water in the radiator and fuel in the tank will behave during race conditions. The general aim is to avoid any unpleasant surprises once you get to the track.

Unfortunately, a nasty shock might not always come in the form of an underperforming component. Back in 2009, the Brawn GP team had survived the Honda pull-out, managed to keep the race-winning potential of the car under wraps (which, incidentally, says a lot about how well they can keep a secret in Formula One) and been to an impressive pre-season test. Against all the odds, they had made it to the first race of the year, only to find that their car was considered by some to be illegal. It all came down to that double diffuser, and the teams who hadn't pursued that route were appealing to the sport's governing body – the Fédération Internationale de l'Automobile (FIA) – to have the part outlawed.

Let's be clear about one thing: at the core of it, Formula One is made up of a group of designers and engineers who are all interpreting the same set of rules and bringing their own reading of what is possible to the table. Almost every team has a dreamer whose role is to consider the far-fetched and try and make it beneficial to an F1 car. Ross Brawn is one such person; he's won titles with Benetton, Ferrari and Brawn GP because not only does he have an incredibly clever and methodical approach to car design, but he's also not afraid to embrace the radical. Radical is just what his Brawn GP car was and, after winning the first two races of 2009, the results were put to the FIA, under appeal. The case was heard in April and would have been an extraordinarily nerve-wracking time for everyone connected to the team. They'd spent the last six months worrying that they wouldn't have jobs for the season, and now after the most impressive start it looked as though they could lose it all. Eventually, after plenty of deliberation, a verdict was delivered: the design was legal, the results would stand and the Brawn GP001 survived an early scare to go on and win the World Championship – in a big way thanks to that innovative double diffuser, and the money and man-hours invested in its development.

It is easy to underestimate the importance of development in Formula One. Quite simply, if the car that won the first race of the season isn't improved, honed and developed throughout the year, then by the end of that season that car would be dead last. You see examples of this constant evolution at every race. Often a team will have a member of the crew fly out to a circuit as late as possible just so they can continue working at the factory until the very last minute to bring the latest updates to the track. It sounds incredible, but I've seen car parts that F1 teams have spent months working on being stowed in the luggage hold next to my bag of spare underwear, so that when we land at our next destination, brand-new parts can be seen rolling around on the baggage reclaim – huge brown boxes with FRAGILE written along the side and team stickers plastered over them. We're talking everything from wings to side pods to floors to wing mirrors – no part of an F1 car is ever considered complete. In 2009, for example, when Renault were struggling, they reportedly took the seats out of Flavio Briatore's private plane in order to fly a new floor out to the Grand Prix. Very F1, don't you think?

But while teams like Renault, Toyota, BMW and Honda can enter the sport and spend vast sums on designing and developing the next radical component, and while Red Bull can rock up and receive billions in funding from owner Dietrich Mateschitz, smaller privateer teams such as Williams are often swimming against the tide. They don't have global car sales or a fizzy drink brand to support their efforts; they simply exist to race, and all they can do is offer their sponsors a spot on the side of the car. And the better they do, the more valuable that advertising spot becomes. In 1979, only the Williams team's third year, they won five races and came second in the championship. The following year the title was theirs. Now contrast that with modern Formula One: teams such as Caterham, Marussia and HRT have been racing for three years yet they haven't won a single point, let alone a race. In the two seasons after Brawn GP won the title, only three teams shared wins: Ferrari, McLaren and Red Bull. The cost to remain competitive in Formula One is ever-increasing, and those three have something in common: massive budgets.

In the eighties and nineties, Williams were legendary multiple champions, and although Sir Frank Williams was left paralysed from the neck down after a tragic car accident in 1986, it is clear just how much he still lives for motorsport. I'm lucky enough to have had the chance to visit most of the F1 teams' factories, but certainly one of the most enlightening was a trip to the Williams HQ. Not only was I shown around their modern F1 facility in Grove, just 30 minutes north of the M4, but I was also lucky enough to be given a tour of their museum and to meet one of my Formula One heroes.

The Williams factory itself stands just feet from a busy road on the outskirts of an Oxfordshire village and if you didn't know what the building housed you might imagine it's a call centre, a council's out-of-town offices or a logistics centre for some heavy-goods company. You'd certainly never think that it builds Formula One cars. On the day of my visit, as I approached down the driveway and swung into my parking bay, I knew this was going to be a big day. I walked into reception and was immediately greeted by one of the glorious creations of yesteryear. Sitting quietly in the centre of the room was one of the greatest cars the team had ever built: designed by Adrian Newey, it was the Williams FW14B, which in 1992 had powered Nigel Mansell to the F1 world title. I've touched cars driven by Alain Prost, Ayrton Senna and Jim Clark, and it still amazes me that the steering wheel, the seatbelts, nuts, bolts and wheels are the very ones that were raced in their illustrious heyday. For me, it's a stark reminder of how transient life is; while we get frail and old, and pass away, these cars remain exactly as they always were, a reminder of past glories.

The factory is a collection of eighties redbrick buildings that would once have seemed at the cutting edge of archi-tectural design. While it now looks like any other office block across the country, once inside you can feel the love and the passion that has carried the team to so much success over the years, and there are constant reminders that you are somewhere special: boardrooms named after classic drivers, circuits or corners; security swipecards needed to move just about anywhere; and emotive photographs on the walls plus trophies on side cabinets as reminders of the team's many triumphs.

Having been wowed by the cars in the factory and taken on a tour of the museum that transported me back to my teenage years watching Williams dominate F1, it was really special to get Frank's personal take on how the sport has changed over the decades. For someone like Frank, who used a phone box to make business calls in the early years before rising to the top, I imagined it must be hard to retain the passion and drive when the costs involved are so large. But in spite of the commercial and financial pressures, Williams continue to do all they can to compete with the current pacesetters; their attention to detail and determination to return to winning form is quite apparent in their design process, which I was talked through using the example of a new front wing design.

Throughout the Formula One season, the head of aerodynamics at Williams will sit with his team and discuss the latest raft of developments and updates. To help the design team create a part that could make a real difference to the performance of the car, they will run it through what is called a

47

Computational Fluid Dynamics (CFD) programme. As aero-dynamics is one of the most significant influences on an F1 car's performance, CFD is used to study how airflow will operate best under, around and over the vehicle, with the aim of disturbing the air as little as possible.

The programme is by no means a basic tool: the engineers can use the software to divide components of the car into specific grids or cells and apply mathematical equations to the information in order to work out how that specific component works. They can also work environmental factors, road surfaces and changing wind conditions into their sums. CFD can split a car into 300 million separately measured points and then assess the car in great detail, sometimes taking almost a day to do one configuration. These programmes are in turn powered by a 'super-computer', which is something a little more impressive than a home PC. In fact, they're so powerful that some of the teams have a separate generator for them, as the mains power just doesn't provide the energy they require. Each super-computer is usually a minimum of twenty teraflops, a teraflop being a measure of how quickly a computer can carry out a mathematical operation. One teraflop equates to one trillion operations per second, so just imagine what a twenty- or thirty-teraflop computer can achieve. Mind-boggling numbers.

Once the Williams team is happy with the results from their CFD programme, they will next create a scale model of the improved part – in this case, the front wing. The front wing is an essential piece of a successful F1 car, as it controls how the wind will flow over the rest of the car, affecting aerodynamic performance for the rest of the wind's journey under, over and around the bodywork. The team create an exact 60 per cent scale model of the new component, which is beautifully crafted by skilled factory workers. Even at this stage, the team might find there is no gain from the new part and end up throwing it away if it's not better than what is already on the car. Only a few parts from hundreds of potential upgrades pass the test, but it's important to remember that this is still a trial and error process. The important question in F1 design isn't just, 'Is the new part better?' but also, 'How does it react with the rest of the car and does it compromise a piece that is already in place?' If they're lucky, the update will improve the car by somewhere between 1 and 3 per cent. F1 is so competitive these days that sometimes a part that improves the car by only half a tenth of a second will be built and raced. Not a simple process, but one that happens behind the doors of F1 team HQs every day of the week.

If Williams decide their update is good enough to take to an F1 race, next comes the carbon-fibre stage. Carbon fibre is the material of choice in modern F1; it may be one of the most expensive materials in the world but it's incredibly light and remarkably tough, perfect for the stresses and strains that it will be placed under in racing conditions. The carbon-fibre elements are moulded, then placed in a giant autoclave that bakes the new update until it's cooked to perfection. Once out of the oven, it's time to assemble the new part, which can take around three days to do by hand. Having fitted the new part into the jigsaw puzzle of the car, the paint is now applied. The paint on an F1 car is about 3 microns thick – that's 0.003mm – and is applied while the bodywork is electrically charged. Nothing is normal in F1!

It's then off to the track, and time for the driver to give his feedback. At this point the testing and evaluating still haven't finished, as the team may apply flo-viz paint to the new part – this can be either a fluorescent paint, or an invisible paint that only shows up under UV light. They will spray the new part, send it to the track and then see where the paint has moved. This will show the direction of the airflow over the car and whether the new part is performing out on the track as well as in theory. All the time they will be cross-referencing the results with what they expected the new part to deliver all those weeks ago back at the factory and in the wind tunnel.

If you're lucky, the car is quicker; not so lucky and the driver might hit the wall just a few corners around the track, making all that hard work count for nothing in the end. So next time you see carbon fibre scattered across the race track, just think of the effort a team like Williams will have put into the making of that part, all in the name of speed.

It's a sobering thought, though, that even if the part is an improvement, the driver is happy and it moves the team up the grid in a race, it's most likely already obsolete. The same process would have started afresh back at base a few days before, as the car continuously evolves throughout the season. Over the course of the season only 30 per cent of the car will remain the same. Constant change, constant evolution, constant improvement.

Yet, even with incredible expertise and vast budgets, updating and improving a Formula One car isn't easy. The 2011 season taught a particularly important lesson to two of the biggest names in F1, McLaren and Ferrari. At the start of the year, I was keeping a close eye on the latest news from the pre-season tests. Unlike in years gone by, there isn't unlimited testing in Formula One – once there was a time when a driver would fly from a race, to a test, to a race, to a test, all season long. These days, testing is restricted to a few days at the start of the season and for this reason it's vital to have a car that is fast right from the off. That year, the latest McLaren car was really struggling. I remember a downcast Jenson Button giving an interview at the end of one of the test days and, when asked how the car was performing, his answer was very frank: 'We haven't done as much running as we'd have liked. I think our reliability's not as good as we'd have hoped. So not so great . . .'

But what was it that had gone wrong? F1 isn't simply a racing battle on the track, it's also an engineering contest off the track and there are times when making the brave, bold and unexpected decisions can pay off. Perhaps McLaren were hoping to emulate Brawn GP's success with the double diffuser and spring a surprise for 2011 – it eventually transpired that they'd designed a system of rather complicated exhausts, which in the words of team principal Martin Whitmarsh 'were not delivering sufficient benefits for their complexity'. In their quest to gain an edge over their rivals, and having been beaten to the title the season before, McLaren were trying something new. There's no doubt they would have put it through the same rigorous procedures as other teams were applying, but it goes to show that in Formula One you never truly know how a car will perform until you put it on the road. In real life, you would never dream of buying a car and driving your family around in it if it had never been road-tested, but that's what the drivers do every time they slide behind the wheel and into the tight confines of a Formula One cockpit. The car has never been tested for real, and only a few races into the new season there are so many new bits that once again it's essentially a prototype. Every F1 car is.

So, the 2011 McLaren was a prototype that wasn't delivering what the team wanted, and McLaren's next move was a real display of their skills, their expertise and their ability to spend money when they need to. The team was no doubt helped by the delay resulting from the cancellation of the Bahrain Grand Prix, which meant the season started two weeks later; even so, when they arrived in Melbourne for the start of the 2011 Formula One season, they performed a near miracle.

An F1 car must possess two very different skills. Of course it must be capable of incredible raw speed, clearly vital given it's a speed-driven sport, but there is not just one way to get to the end of a race first, and it involves more than simply having the fastest car. Some cars are fast, but are made more unstable than others by the amount of fuel they have on board or are slowed by having greater tyre degradation; others are slower than their rivals but are so stable and easy on their tyres that they can make minimal pit stops and gain numerous points. The F1 weekend tests all of a car's skills. In qualifying it's minimum fuel, raw pace that is tested. Once the race starts it's what is called 'race pace', and the test is of a driver's ability to keep the pace up as the race unfolds around them.

Having clearly finished pre-season testing with their tails between their legs, the McLaren team returned to the factory and proceeded to redesign the parts of their car that were letting them down. I recall heading to the garage and looking at the frantically reworked McLaren, and as it sat on the track in Melbourne it was possible to see where the changes had been made. The team, who had clearly been working until the very last moment to update and improve their charge, hadn't even had time to finish the car properly. Usually, as much effort is put into the aesthetic appearance of a car as it is into performance, particularly when it comes to McLaren, a team who deal in perfection. Yet on this occasion, the rear of the McLaren, around the diffuser and suspension rods, looked unlike any other car; it almost looked unfinished, an indication of just how late in the day they were making changes – and remember, they also had to allow time to ship these new parts to the other side of the world. Nevertheless, those frantic efforts proved worth it as that opening weekend, in qualifying, a car that had been well off the pace in pre-season testing ended up second and fourth on the grid, with only the Red Bull cars proving to be faster.

As for the race itself, Sebastian Vettel was on pole and made a great start, while the McLarens of Lewis Hamilton and Jenson Button started slowly from second and fourth. Vettel was unchallenged into the first corner, and Hamilton kept second from Webber. Button was unable to defend his position as he was under pressure and dropped to sixth behind Felipe Massa. Seb led at the end of the first lap, but Lewis was closing the gap and keeping hold of second. With the race moving into its final phase, Lewis slid off the track at the first corner and damaged the underside of his car. It was enough to stop him from mounting a serious challenge for Vettel's top spot, but he did keep his McLaren in second place despite being chased down by Fernando Alonso and Mark Webber. Although it will go down as the victory for Sebastian Vettel that started his championship-winning year, McLaren will also remember it as the time they went from struggling just to complete a race distance in testing to having both cars in the points and Lewis Hamilton on the podium.

It was some achievement, but then you only need to pay a

visit to their phenomenal HQ to see that being better, faster, stronger and more successful than their rivals clearly runs in McLaren's DNA. I don't think I've ever visited anywhere quite like the McLaren Technology Centre, and I'll never forget my first trip. Pulling off the roundabout near Woking, in Surrey, I got my first taste of the perfection and attention to detail that course through the veins of the team as I passed the silver and grey McLaren sign and stopped at the security hut. I call it a security 'hut', but in fact it was a two-storey building, with sliding doors, white tiled floors and chrome everywhere. I gave my name to the two immaculately presented security guards, who then produced a map for me – not an old dog-eared paper affair, but a work of art in itself. White, laminated, resplendent. I was directed towards a VIP entrance, and as I approached I saw that one of the buildings in the complex was in fact built into the side of a valley, with the roof covered in grass. I felt like I was walking through a James Bond film.

New saplings and a wetland area to my left were teeming with wildlife, and to my right was a huge lake, out of which the place the McLaren team call home seemed to rise. It was a vast, perfectly curved structure, all glass and steel, and even more remarkable was the fact that there was not a smear or a scratch in sight. Perfection.

As I entered through two massive, silently sliding doors, my breath was taken away. It wasn't the walkways crisscrossing above me high in the atrium, or the huge trophy cabinet at the far end of the room, or the engineers working away in impossibly clean, sealed workshops where the F1 cars were being built. What had caught me off-guard were the F1 cars stretched out before me, from one of founder Bruce McLaren's early race cars to Lewis Hamilton's championship-winning car of 2008 and everything in between. Talk about a way to inspire your staff! Cars driven by the likes of Ayrton Senna, Alain Prost and Mika Hakkinen filled what I now know to be called 'the Boulevard'. It's a constant reminder of what McLaren have achieved, of the high standards that are expected of anyone working for the team and of the ultimate aim – to create champions.

The building is predominantly grey, and extremely quiet, so that you find yourself whispering and feeling rather under-dressed. It's incredibly impressive. At the end of the Boulevard is a trophy cabinet that stretches further than the length of my house – it's also strategically positioned to be the thing that all the staff walk past on their way to lunch, in case they needed any reminding. Every door needs a security pass to open it and the only sounds you can hear are heels clicking on perfectly polished tiles and the whoosh of automatic doors opening up as people go about their business.

McLaren's 'Mission Control' completely blew me away. At a race weekend, there will be a pit-wall team, with the team boss and the race engineers right next to the action. Millions of pounds are spent on sensors for the cars, process-ing thousands of pieces of data at all times, and during a race weekend up to fifty samples of oil can be taken from the cars and analysed, sometimes in laboratories that are actually at the race track. That way, if there is an issue with the fuel or the oil it can be rectified there and then; the traces of metal in the oil offer important indications as to the state of the engine. All this information is fed back to Mission Control, and it is here that decisions are made, information is analysed and race strategy and car performance information is pored over, no matter how many thousands of miles away the race might be.

On down another silent, gleaming, modern corridor was another amazing room, the McLaren Simulator. I was lucky enough to be shown inside by Jenson, but as the contents of the room are a closely guarded secret, the only interesting piece of information I can share with you here is that during a race weekend, the teams have reserve and test drivers working away in the simulator. But why, you might ask, when you have race drivers in their cars on an actual track, do you want a young driver doing the same thing on a simulator? This is a fascinating example of just how important the role of the factory is over the race weekend. Imagine the team at the track are considering a fundamental change to the set-up of the car that might take time to implement. In a simulator, to make a significant change to the front wing, the steering rack or the exhaust system takes a few clicks on a keyboard; the change can then be 'driven' and the results fed back. These simulators are so much more than computer games – by changing the set-up details on the 'car', the driver in the simulator can give real insights into how it alters the way a vehicle handles, and how much grip or downforce they have. It's also important that the reserve driver knows what the race drivers like. That way, they can try a new part and say, 'Jenson will like that' or, 'It is good but won't work with Fernando's driving style.'

And it doesn't stop there. The F1 simulators are so sophisticated and sensitive that they can even help teams decide which tyres to use, and how long to stay on those tyres. So, the trackside team send all the information they have gained back to the factory, along with an idea of how they will approach the race and the best strategy to employ. The team on the simulator will then conduct a race with that information at their disposal, and the simulator will give an accurate picture of how the race may unfold – how the tyres perform, how the degradation or temperature affects their performance and, ultimately, whether the race team are making the right decisions.

It's a constant process over the entire race weekend. On Fridays at a Grand Prix, you have first practice in the morning, followed by the second practice session in the afternoon. However, when the cars are off the track between the two sessions, back in the simulator the factory-based team can run a variety of different set-up changes so that by the time the afternoon session gets underway the team are already a step ahead. Friday is a crucial day at a Grand Prix, to get the car 'hooked in' to the track.

However, that isn't where it ends. Even before heading off to a race weekend the drivers can spend hours familiarising themselves with the next track on the calendar; and the team can even put 'virtual upgrades' on a simulator to see if the driver likes the changes before they go to the effort of taking them to the track. If he does like what he's 'virtually driving', those changes can be implemented on his actual race car.

The simulator is also an essential tool for the reserve drivers to get some time behind the wheel. With in-season testing so limited, it provides the ideal opportunity for teams to assess the skills of a young driver – who will experience the genuine effects of g-forces on the body and the physical challenges of driving the car – and see if they have the potential to step up to a race seat. In return, those young drivers will use the simulator and all the tools at their disposal to help the race team to victory thousands of miles away. If you think the celebrations on the podium are intense, you can be sure they are just as emotional back at base, well away from the world's media and the TV cameras. I wish I could tell you more about how the simulators look and what technology the teams are employing. But this is a highly sensitive area and I'm sworn to secrecy!

Last on my magical mystery tour was the gym. Resembling a high-end London affair, it had all the toys you can imagine, along with a pool to make sure the staff are fully relaxed before designing components that might just deliver another Formula One world title.

As I said goodbye to my hosts and the glass doors slid open for my departure, as I returned along the pristine path, past the serene lake and back to a security hut that could win an architecture prize, I was struck by the apparent contrast between McLaren's Technology Centre and the Ferrari base in Maranello. Whereas the MTC celebrates modernity and clean lines with its very sterile approach, Maranello is full of passion, history and reverence. But it would be foolish to think that Ferrari's more mundane exterior and classically Italian approach to their HQ means they pay any less attention to detail. I've been there twice now, and both times I've been asked to walk in rather than drive. Why would an F1 team not embrace a car? Because my chosen hire car wasn't part of the Fiat Group and, in the eyes of Ferrari, that's a no-no. It's a small point in many ways, but for me it sums up the competitive nature and partisan attitude to the sport that all the teams demonstrate. In F1, it seems, you're either a team member or an opponent; there is no middle ground.

The Ferrari HQ is a fascinating place. The success the team has enjoyed for decades hasn't been through luck. Although it feels very different to the home of McLaren, as with MTC, everywhere you go there are reminders of an illustrious past, from roads named after Ferrari F1 champions to the very farmhouse that Enzo Ferrari used as his office when he ran the team. The Maranello factory has been the base since Enzo transferred the operation from nearby Modena, and his office has been left exactly as it was in his day. It is with great pride that the current members of the team will allow you to have a look around a building that means so much to them.

While I was having a look around, I went up to the boardroom where I saw a picture of the signing of the first ever Concorde Agreement, which dictates the terms on which teams compete in races and take their share of revenue and prize money. The very room I was in would have played a crucial part in the discussions and negotiations, and as I was taking it all in a tanned figure appeared, wearing only a jockstrap. It was a certain Fernando Alonso, who had just been having a rubdown in one of the small rooms in the old building. He was more than happy to stand and chat despite his state of undress – but if my body resembled his then I imagine I'd feel just as confident!

It's difficult to explain really just how different the pressure is on Ferrari in Italy. I guess the most accurate description is to call them the national team of Italy. The entire town of Maranello is dedicated to Ferrari: you can hire supercars in the small town centre for a lap around the town; you can visit the Ferrari Museum, where fans can get up close and personal with the cars; and from almost every house and out of every bedroom window you will see hanging a black prancing horse. Against this backdrop, it's not hard to imagine the pressure on the team to win not just races but championships. But in F1 it simply isn't that easy, and even with the benefits of CFD, wind tunnels and flo-viz paint testing, it's still far from an exact science. In 2011 the Ferrari team learned exactly how inexact that science could be.

At the start of the season the results weren't what the team were expecting. Having finished third in the championship in 2010 they wanted, and needed, to hit the ground running the following season. However, three races into the year and they'd not even managed a podium, with a solitary fourth place their best result. Ferrari were designing cars that they thought were going to be fast and competitive, yet when their upgrades made it to the track they didn't seem to improve the performance. It was puzzling and frustrating to say the least, until at last the mystery was solved by an investigation of their wind tunnel. As we've seen, wind tunnels are extremely important pieces of machinery in the development of an F1 car, but you have to trust what they are telling you. The problem was that Ferrari's wind tunnel was telling them one thing when the reality was quite different. Therefore the team had to undertake a thorough review, and used the Toyota wind tunnel in Cologne for a time to provide a benchmark from which they could assess theirs before eventually recalibrating their own machinery.

The issue was eventually sorted, and though it may have only been relatively minor, it nevertheless hampered Ferrari's start to 2011. In F1 you can't afford to give any of your rivals a free pass, and bearing in mind that there are only twenty races in a season, performing badly in two races equates to 10 per cent of your season falling by the wayside.

It just goes to show that much of what happens in Formula

The sport that never sleeps

One is determined by what takes place behind the closed doors of the team HQs, and there's no doubt that most races are won and lost in such places. The sport is more cut-throat, competitive and technologically advanced than ever before. From the drivers at the top of the pyramid to the engineers back at the factory, F1 is really only driven by one thing: the constant search for speed in the relentless pursuit of victory.

3

The dynamics of an F1 team

One of the driving forces in Formula One is the collective pride that comes from being part of a team. It's always clear when working with ex-F1 personnel that pride and teamwork are paramount, and that is why uniforms are such an important part of pit-lane life. For someone like me, who is rubbish with names, the uniforms are a real boon as most have their owner's moniker emblazoned on them somewhere. Just as with a football team, donning the uniform breeds not only an atmosphere of 'them and us', but also a sense of belonging and a duty to uphold standards – there's no hiding place when you can be instantly identified by what you are wearing.

Many of the former F1 employees who turn their hand to

broadcasting actually find it a little odd that in 'everyday life' people don't all have to wear exactly what their employer tells them to. The average F1 employee is kitted out in tops, trousers, trainers, even watches, as specified by the team. All of them perfectly clean, all of them updated most seasons. Even when travelling to the airport, or flying to the other side of the world, they are expected to be representing the team properly by what they wear. From constantly polishing a car even when it's raining to painting the tyres of the F1 trucks black when they arrive at a race, to offering the cleanest, best-presented motorhome in the paddock, it's part of the pursuit of perfection that runs through the sport. It is also a reminder that everyone is pulling in the same direction. The race outfit represents that team and their driver, and with wearing it comes a certain amount of responsibility. I imagine it must be awe-inspiring, whatever your job, to look around and see everyone in the same, perfect attire, almost like an army.

I attended a corporate event with Lewis Hamilton a few years ago and we both had to get changed. While I just pulled off my clothes and slung them over a chair, Lewis carefully removed his and folded them neatly, before checking his hair in the mirror more than once! However, among the drivers that attention to detail seems to be the norm and is one of the reasons I think they all love Japan as a race destination. It is a country where order and control are supreme – a perfect setting for F1, where obsession over minutiae is the expected standard. I've actually found it incredibly inspiring and for me it's a reminder that, whatever your walk of life, making every small part of it as perfect and impressive as possible can bring great rewards. As Churchill once said, 'A living is about what you get, a life is about what you give.'

The magic of teamwork in F1 is built on many things, not least a belief that by working together anything is possible. This was evident in 2012 when Fernando Alonso and Ferrari dragged their car to the top of the championship standings by mid-season. Why was this noteworthy? Because at the start of the year the team were 2 seconds off the pace. But this is much more than just another story about a team working hard in the factory to bridge the gap. It's about how one driver can inspire the men around him. Since he joined Ferrari, Fernando Alonso has moulded the team around him, regularly spending time with his mechanics and engineers, playing football with them after a hard day's work at Maranello and never failing to give them the credit when success finally came.

It was in the second race of 2012 that Fernando put the team's pre-season woes behind them by winning a remarkable rain-soaked Malaysian Grand Prix. When you look at the stats of that race, it was probably Fernando's greatest win, as at the time the Ferrari was still some way off the pace of the leaders. However, he dealt with the slippery track, kept his rival Sergio Perez in the Sauber at bay and as he crossed the line his race engineer, Andrea Stella, described it as 'the most beautiful'. It was in complete contrast to the despair at the start of the year, the meetings, the scrutiny, the questions about how a great team could have got it so wrong in development over the winter. Imagine then that even before you've had a chance to fully improve the car, you see your lead driver perform a near-miracle to take a win. Now think how much of a boost that would have been to those at the factory, the men and women working all hours to improve things. Suddenly, they know that if they give Fernando a car that has a chance of scoring points or winning, then he will deliver. It generates a feeling that nothing is pointless, that every little bit of improvement will be exploited to the max.

And this is why I say that the driver sits at the top of the pyramid. There are plenty of people who can do each other's job at the factory, many with the skills and knowledge to run a race from the pit wall, but few who can do what a driver does. If someone further down the pyramid doesn't do their job, it's unfortunate; if the driver doesn't do his, then it's often critical. There is nowhere to hide for the driver; his responsibility is to deliver the race on behalf of the hundreds of people who have got the car to that point. And I guess that's why it's particularly hard when a driver is no longer considered good enough. When they are fast the team revolves around them. They are lauded, celebrated and congratulated. As soon as the speed is no longer there, the media and fans lose interest and the team bosses lose patience.

The role of the team principal is also key. They not only have to drive the team from a technical point of view, but also a human one, and it's often hard for the two to go hand-in-hand. In my experience, people who are very technically gifted, great mathematicians, designers or strategists, are not necessarily inspirational leaders of men. Imagine if you are Christian Horner at Red Bull or Stefano Domenicali at Ferrari. You need to understand the fundamentals of the car's design, trust that it is within the spirit and the limits of the rules. You have to build a technical team that can operate at the highest level and make sure that the whole team from bottom to top are as disciplined and committed as possible. You have to instil a spirit of 'them and us' to make sure sensitive information is kept in-house and the team are inspired to give their working lives to the cause. Then you need to be a great communicator, not just in dealing with the media and the scrutiny that comes with the job, but also in motivating the team and keeping the drivers happy.

You might argue that keeping the drivers happy should be easy enough. After all, two men who love racing are being paid a small fortune to drive the fastest cars in the world. Well, inter-driver rivalry is legendary in Formula One, and that's the way we like it. Remember, the driver's teammate is the only person in the field who has identical equipment, so therefore identical chances of success. This engenders a deep desire to beat your teammate. I've been told by one very famous F1 driver that he'd rather 'finish fifteenth but in front of my teammate than him to win it and me to be second'. This attitude leads to the most intense rivalries, with drivers making sure they fight for their position within the team. For years rumours have circulated about certain drivers having clauses in their contracts that explicitly state they are the number-one driver and should get preferential treatment.

It falls to the team principal to keep two fiercely competitive drivers happy. At McLaren most people are amazed that a duo of world champions can co-exist so harmoniously. However, I think even Lewis and Jenson would admit they aren't best mates. You need to keep a distance for the rivalry to remain fired up. Usually it happens that a strong driver is paired with a teammate who is often seen to be there to help the number-one driver. Just look at the famous time Ferrari's Rubens Barrichello moved over for Michael Schumacher in Austria in 2002, which sparked international condemnation, or the questions faced by the same team when Fernando Alonso was allowed to slip past by Felipe Massa in Germany in 2010. It's a fine balance to have two drivers with equal status and can lead to some rather public spats.

Just think back to 2010 at Silverstone, when Red Bull had an updated front wing but only two of them available. Before the race Sebastian Vettel's wing broke. This presented a huge dilemma for the team. At the time Sebastian was ahead of Mark Webber in the title battle, but only by a slim margin of twelve points. The team took a big decision and for qualifying gave Vettel the updated front wing belonging to Webber. Imagine Mark's reaction when he was subsequently outqualified by such a small margin that you could argue the new part had made all the difference. So there was plenty of attention on the two drivers when they lined up first and second on the grid the following day. As the race started Mark and Seb were going wheel to wheel, with the Australian coming out on top after his young teammate got a puncture when trying to go around the outside of Webber at the first corner. I'll never forget the words Mark uttered as he crossed the line to win the race: 'Not bad for a number two driver.' Not only was this making his feelings crystal clear to the team, but I'm sure he was well aware the message would also be broadcast to millions of race fans.

In the event, Sebastian went on to take the championship that season, and the two are still teammates now. However, it serves to illustrate how at any time just one decision from the bosses can have catastrophic effects within the team.

One of the ways of keeping morale up is by celebrating with those who put so much in but who don't get to enjoy the buzz of the pit lane. Only a lucky few employees from each team actually get to travel to the races; the rest do the hard work and watch the race unfold on TV. Therefore, it's a lovely tradition that the winning driver will often fly back to the factory on the day after a race or a title win, to share the moment with the hundreds of people who may be far from the action but are made to feel part of the team. It's another way in which the management endeavours to make the whole venture as inclusive as possible.

For a sport that relies so heavily on teamwork, it is

somewhat ironic that only rarely do all the parts that make up an F1 team come together. Most of the year, the test team based at the factory are trying out thousands of different improvements, subjecting them to umpteen tests to see how they will react at a race weekend, with only the very best and most rewarding upgrades making the cut. The race team are concentrating on their side of the bargain, which is to turn up to each event, build the garage, prepare the car and make sure that from an engineering perspective, each race weekend runs like clockwork. Then there is the driver, who, over the course of the season, actually spends only between sixty and eighty days at Grands Prix, and a remarkably low total of around forty hours a year actually competing in F1 races – astonishing when you consider that those few hours, less than two days, define their year and often their career. And finally you have the management who are busy juggling the financial, business side of racing, and the actual on-track activity. All of these separate components make up a modern F1 team, and a pit stop is just about the only time they all come together.

With no refuelling currently allowed in Formula One, pit stops are quicker than they've ever been. A loud, aggressive ballet dance that is over in less than 3 seconds if it's good. A few seconds that can make or break a race. Pit stops involve everyone: the senior race engineer, usually in consultation with the team principal, will have a discussion about tactics; the team back at the factory will have been working on the simulator and their computers until late the night before, also trying to formulate the best race strategy. The driver, too, has had to play his part. F1 tyres are so fragile that the driver knows the strategy in advance, and he must drive to that plan. For example, if the team have decided on a three-stop strategy, then the driver knows that he may have to stop more often, but in between times he can punish his tyres as he'll get through four sets of rubber. Alternatively, if there has been a team decision to make it a one-stop race, the driver will know his job is to eke out the life of the tyres, not to push it too hard at the start of the race otherwise they will wear out too quickly, he'll have to stop too early and that will mean longer on the second set. The result of this mistake is often a disaster all round: usually the driver, while wearing out his tyres a lap or two early, still hasn't actually gone as fast as those who had always planned to make two stops from the start. The frustration is that the team will need to stop twice, but the driver hasn't gone at the optimum pace. Next, the mechanics come into play. They know when to expect their driver in, what tyres he is going to use next, and what other changes, if any, he is expecting.

Cue the decision from the pit wall: 'Box this lap.' The strategists back at the factory and at the track hold their breath, the driver holds his nerve as he scorches into the pit lane, careful not to break the 100kph speed limit. The race engineer barks some last-minute instructions to the driver or the pit crew, and then suddenly it's over. Everyone has played their part, and if the strategy, the pit-stop time and the driver's skill have all worked out, it can mean the difference between a race won and a race lost. In recent seasons we've seen this more and more as tyres have struggled for life. In fact, in mid-2012 Mercedes and Red Bull both said they were going to spend less time working on aerodynamics and put their energy into understanding the F1 tyres, as that is where races are currently being decided.

I actually got to experience just how brave the pit-stop boys are when I had a go at changing a wheel at Silverstone a few years ago. I was working for CBBC at the time and the team called Spyker (now Force India) were testing at the home of the British Grand Prix. I was given the job of rear-wheel jack-man, and had no idea what it was like to kneel on the floor while holding heavy equipment that means you can't leap out of the way if you need to . . . and then for an F1 car travelling at 100kph to aim straight at you. There is incredible trust involved, as to hit the marks and make it a quick stop the front wing and wheels pass just inches from the mechanics. And these guys aren't paid millions to risk their lives like the drivers. They might earn £50,000 a year if they're extremely lucky – not exactly a private-jet, champagne lifestyle!

Having felt the fear as the F1 car slows from 100kph to zero in just a few feet, having dealt with the adrenaline surge you get as the stop is unfolding and then been hit by the wall of heat as the car shoots out of the pit lane, I have nothing but massive respect for the mechanics and engineers in Formula One – not least because my stop was about 15 seconds and that was the best I could do!

An F1 car is made up of, on average, 5,000 pieces. Therefore, if it were assembled 99 per cent correctly, it would still start a race with fifty things wrong! If one of those parts not assembled properly was the water hose, and it were to blow off, the car's complete cooling system would empty in just over a second. That would be race over. Once built and at a Grand Prix, in the middle of a race the car will scorch into the pits. It's such a stressful environment for mechanics that some of the teams employ psychologists to teach their pit crew relaxation techniques and help them deal with the very brief but dramatic peak. Once a pit stop is called they may start deep breathing and even perform hand exercises to make sure their reactions are on the money. You can understand why. In the three short seconds a pit stop lasts the following happens: four tyres are removed and replaced by new ones; side pods, essential for cooling, are cleared out if blocked; a driver's set-up might require changes, so the front wing might be given a couple of turns with a screwdriver; any suspected damage is inspected; the car is released into the pit lane without hindering those around it or compromising another team on their way in.

A 3-second whirlwind, and the performance of that crew can be decisive. And this is perhaps the biggest lesson of all to grasp: F1 is the ultimate sport of trust – trust in your teammate, trust in your mechanics, trust in the designers. If anyone at any stage doesn't do their job properly, the result can be disastrous. F1 is a sport of such fine margins the slightest mistake can prove very costly indeed. In Hockenheim in 2012 the McLaren team recorded what many believe to be the fastest pit stop on record at that time. Jenson Button was stationary in the pits for just 2.31 seconds. A remarkable feat, but it's also worth remembering that at such speeds it's easy to make mistakes. At the following race at Silverstone, the cut and thrust was too much for Kamui Kobayashi, who seemed to misjudge his speed as he entered the pits, skidding into a number of his pit crew who were waiting to change his tyres. Thankfully the injuries weren't life-threatening.

Fans often perceive F1 as a battle of driver versus driver, an individual sport where only one man can be crowned world champion and is given hero status. Yet if you look a little deeper, you'll see that in fact it's the exact opposite – it's the greatest team sport. It's taken hundreds of people thousands of man-hours to design, construct and test a car that is considered worthy to race in a Formula One Grand Prix, but it's when that car arrives at the circuit that the real teamwork begins.

While the designers and wind-tunnel engineers are back at base immediately after a Grand Prix, working on updates to the car and processing information, some of the team members are at the next circuit a full week before the race. Team bosses, drivers and PR people will usually arrive at a race two days before cars are on track, but the car itself and a whole army of other crew will have been hard at work for days, often having travelled directly from the last race. For most people a Formula

One weekend lasts a couple of hours on a Sunday afternoon, between the lights going out for the race start and the winner crossing the line. True, this is the pinnacle; the crescendo where every point of the drivers' and constructors' championship is won and lost, but it's by no means the whole picture.

Those a little more obsessed with F1 may also tune into the qualifying session the day before. At some of the F1 circuits overtaking can be so tricky that the race can almost be won and lost at this part of the weekend. Take circuits such as Monaco or Singapore where the cars race around a built-up, busy city. The track is so narrow and the drivers make mistakes so rarely that although on the TV it looks like it may be possible, overtaking actually takes incredible nerves, bravery and a good slice of luck. Therefore, getting a great position on the grid is an essential part of a successful race weekend and it means the driver and team need to hit the ground running right from the first practice session. A crash caused by driver error on a Friday, or a misjudged strategy from the race team on the Saturday, and it can ruin the weekend before it's really begun.

If we take a moment to look beyond just the race weekend of Saturday and Sunday, here is an insight into the kind of preparation that is going on long before cars are racing for points and position. Traditionally, one of the first races in Europe is also one of the sport's most illustrious, the Monaco Grand Prix. The Monte Carlo race is usually held in early summer, five or six races into the season. If you've never been to Monaco then imagine a little fishing village or perhaps a beautiful hamlet in the Cotswolds or the Highlands of Scotland. Not architecturally speaking, as Monaco is ever evolving and disappointingly modern and ugly, but in terms of the tight, twisting streets, dead ends and confusing one-way systems. And it's busy, incredibly busy. Quite simply, it isn't a place designed to welcome tens of thousands of race fans, hundreds of members of the world's media and an entire fleet of articulated lorries descending annually on the now F1-weary residents. It is often said that if Monaco applied to be an F1 circuit these days it wouldn't meet the strict stand-ards that the modern sport demands. I'm not sure if that is true, nor what part of Monaco fails to come up to scratch, but the following is an idea of what the teams have to deal with logistically once they get there. This is just to get their cars into the garages.

I recall my first trip to the principality and the hour-long drive along the beautiful French Riviera from Nice airport. As you cruise along the motorway, sunglasses on, getting excited about covering one of the blue riband F1 races, you pass a nondescript area of scrubland a few miles outside Monaco. If you look carefully, you will spy the Ferrari, Williams, McLaren or Red Bull wheels parked just off the road and miles from the action. However, they're not the race cars; they are the team lorries and how and why they end up there is quite a story.

For European races such as Monaco the freight arrives in

a fleet of articulated lorries that are driven across the continent and due to arrive a full week before the race actually starts. Now, at most races the lorries, of which there are often four per team, carrying everything from spare team kit and office supplies to the race cars themselves, just turn up, drive into the vast paddock or pit lane and offload. Not in Monaco. Due to the confines of the circuit, the lorries all rendezvous at the dusty car park a few miles out of town and then they actually have pre-assigned delivery slots. The harbour edge where the racing takes place is so claustrophobic that getting a lorry down there is an achievement in itself. Therefore, after trekking thousands of miles across Europe, the teams have to arrive at specifically allocated times, get down to the pit lane, offload their truckful of F1 stuff and then wind their way back through the narrow, famous old streets and back to the car park way out of town. Then it's the next lorry's turn and so on until twenty-four gleaming cars and all the kit are in position.

However, if you think that is tough, a few years ago it was even worse. The cars of the less successful teams used to be kept up the hill in a public car park where they would be race-readied, and then wheeled through the streets to the pit lane. The garages may be small now, but a few years ago they didn't have garages at all! Eddie Jordan gave me a garage tour around the Monaco pit lane once and it was staggering. All the gear that the teams need to run their usually slick F1 operation has to be crammed into a garage that isn't much bigger than a garden shed. There is virtually no room between the cars, and the teams adapt their garage set-up to suit the tight confines – but that's all they can adapt. They still have to build, alter and work on the car as they usually would, perform their super-quick stops in the narrow pit lane, and do it all in a place that is often roastingly hot.

The really unusual aspect of Monaco, however, is out the back of the garages. That is where the paddock is normally situated. In Monaco, however, just about three feet behind the garages, is the actual start–finish straight where the cars are on full throttle and often racing for position as they pass by.

I've chatted to a few of the drivers' physios about it and they describe it as the most daunting race of all. A driver's physio is more than just a fitness expert, nutritionist, masseur, motivator and helmet carrier – he is the driver's right-hand man for the whole weekend. The most you see of a driver's physio is probably when they are on the grid pre-race and he's the man who will never leave that driver's side. I remember once interviewing Jenson Button on the grid, and when we'd finished I wanted to get a word from his physio, Mikey 'Muscles' Collier. As I turned to Mikey, Jenson decided he'd had enough and started to walk off. At this point Mikey found himself in a dilemma: he was about to be interviewed on live television, yet his job was to be at Jenson's beck and call. There was only going to be one winner; he turned on his heels and was gone. After all, Jenson pays his wages – not me!

The two are indicative of the relationship the drivers and their physios enjoy up and down the grid. At a race weekend the physio's job is all about planning the driver's meals, mixing up his energy drinks, working out the right level of exercise to be doing; but, more than that, providing a level of continuity. Imagine your job took you around the globe and your days were filled with media interviews, engineers' briefings and fulfilling sponsor commitments. This is what the drivers routinely do and they need someone by their side. The physios aren't part of the team's management, with high-powered dinners to attend during the evening; they're also not 'one of the lads' in the garage, so they don't go out for a few drinks after work, nor do they socialise with the hangers-on or the media. Therefore, the physio is a steady presence, an important constant in a driver's life, and you will often see them out eating dinner together at a race weekend.

Although it's a team sport, the driver is always slightly separate from the others because he is the only person in that team doing his particular job. Away from the race weekends, driver and physio will again spend plenty of time together – it really is this man's job to make sure that, when the lights go out, the driver is as mentally and physically prepared as he can be. There is one other job that most physios perform: holding the pit boards. A pit board is a fallback in case radio communication fails, and it is a three foot by three foot board that tells the driver where they are relative to their opponents on every lap. Despite the constant radio chatter, many of the drivers have described it as being like a comfort blanket; after all, they've seen pit boards at every level of racing since karting. It's far less of a comfort blanket for the man who has to hold the board out over the race track, however. Very little can really describe how fast an F1 car is actually travelling down the start–finish straight of an F1 track. I always think a good example is to imagine doing 70mph on a motorway and then going three times faster! And it's against this backdrop that the pit boards are lifted up and dangled over the side of the pit wall. I don't think I'd have the nerve – just think if you dropped it!

I recall talking to Mark Webber's pit-wall guy, Rich Connor, after the 2011 Canadian Grand Prix, when Lewis Hamilton and Jenson Button collided down the straight right next to the pit wall. At the time, Rich was holding out the board to relay information to Mark, who was following the McLaren pair. Lewis and Jenson collided; Lewis hit the wall and then made contact with Rich's pit board. If you look at it on the TV you can see the two cars touch; Lewis slews to his left and there are maybe four or five pit boards hanging out over the track. Rich's gets hit and the impact sends shattered bits of the board through the air. They may look light and harmless on TV, but the reality is that a pit board is often made of carbon fibre and it takes quite a whack to break it. In my book you'd need nerves of steel and a fair amount of bravery to keep hold of it in that situation. Rich describes it as a pretty hairy moment, but he wasn't fazed and still works with Mark today.

And that story for me is a further illustration of the one thing that makes the sport tick when everyone comes together at the track: trust – the bedrock of F1 teamwork.

Although the sport's governing body has stringent crash test regulations, it still takes bags of trust to believe that when you turn into a corner at 200mph the car is going to stick to the track. If it doesn't you must also trust that when things go wrong the car will protect you. As each F1 car is effectively a prototype, often never raced before, you can see how big a role trust has to play.

In 2010 at the Chinese Grand Prix the Toro Rosso driver Sebastien Buemi was making his way towards turn 14 in practice when suddenly the most extraordinary accident occurred. Turn 14 in China is a tight right-hand hairpin after a straight of over a kilometre where the cars travel at speeds of over 300kph. At full pelt down that particular straight the loads on the car are incredible, and under braking there is more than 5g of deceleration, the car rolls forwards, the entire load pushed towards the front. Suddenly, bang, both front wheels shot vertically up into the air and bounced away from him down the track. The front of the car in tatters, Buemi was now completely helpless in the cockpit and veered off to the left and into the barriers. When you watch the on-board footage of the car, it's remarkable to see how Buemi managed to retain the presence of mind to steer away from the barrier. Of course, it was a futile action with no front wheels.

Why did this happen? The front of the car was fitted with

brand-new 'uprights', and one of them failed, followed immediately by the other. They were new parts on the car and had never been used before. He was driving a prototype, just like every F1 car. This is a spectacular example of what can happen when a part doesn't perform in the way a team expects, despite extensive, expensive testing. Sometimes it's an aerodynamic part that doesn't deliver extra performance; on other occasions it can be a little more dramatic, as the incident in China proves.

As for Buemi, his response to the media afterwards gave a small insight into a racing driver's psyche. When asked if the accident would dent his confidence, his answer was this: 'Something broke, it happened. We'll change the car and it will be fine so I don't think about it.' What does that show from a driver? Complete trust in his team. And from the men who unload the trucks to the physios who are at the heart of it all to the drivers themselves, it's at the track where you get a real sense of F1 teamwork in action.

Team cohesion is strengthened even more by two important factors: the pursuit of excellence, and the desire to stay one step ahead of the opposition. It's said that to run an F1 team you need to start with a budget of £1.25 million a week, or over £60 million a year. Now this is just the basic figure before you start adding on extra speed. The first £10 million you spend on top of this may well offer big leaps in performance, the next £10 million less so as you are into diminishing returns, so the top teams are laying out huge sums of money, hundreds of millions, to go racing and are spending big cash for what might be tiny gains. Therefore, to get the most out of the considerable investment that F1 represents, everyone at the track needs to know their role and carry it out with perfection and precision – two watchwords of F1.

I recall being on the roof of one of the team homes in Abu Dhabi a couple of years ago and I was chatting to two of the young guys who were working in the team motorhome. Every team has their own hospitality unit at the race, and in Abu Dhabi they are particularly impressive. On the rooftop overlooking the circuit there was an area where guests, the drivers or team members could relax in the Middle Eastern sunshine. However, when I was up there it was the start of the week and they were just getting ready for the guests to arrive. There were a number of large black outdoor chairs and the two young employees were walking around and drawing on the chairs with a black marker pen. I went over for a chat to find out what on earth they were doing, and their answer took me aback. They were drawing over the tiny, almost invisible green stitching on all the chairs – a painstaking and tedious job. 'Why?' I asked. They replied that black was a team colour, but green wasn't and they couldn't possibly have a non-corporate colour on display in their area . . .

Now, on the surface of it, it may seem like complete madness, and on this occasion it may just have been, but that attention to detail is everywhere in this sport and it's often the difference between success and failure. Even when it's wet there are people who spend their time wiping the rain off the shiny silver barriers outside the garages. When the team lorries arrive at the track they are thoroughly washed, the wheels are polished and the tyres are repainted jet black before they are parked in the paddock. When they are parked they are all in a perfect line, not so much as an inch out of place. McLaren even use special stickers on their car these days, which perfectly match the paint job, so that when there are marks or stone chips and no time to send it back to their HQ for a full repaint, they just apply a sticker and the car looks as good as new.

I've actually found the obsession with perfection in F1 quite inspiring. Having spent time with many former drivers, I've noticed how the obsession seems to stay with them, whether it's their homes, where they sit and reflect on their impressive careers, or in their new business ventures after racing. Some may think it's pointless or just showing off, but I honestly think that everything associated with a team is about being the best, matching up to a gold standard, never settling for anything less; then when it comes to things that really matter, that ethos will carry through.

However, you can have all the perfectly pressed uniforms, pristine lorries and spotless garages you like; it'll all count for nothing if you don't win races and show genuine speed. That's what a race weekend is really all about.

Long before guests are being entertained, champagne drunk or millions around the world are tuning in to watch the racing, it's the unglamorous, cold, monotonous world of the pre-season test. F1 teams now have limited pre-season testing – generally, before a season begins they have just twelve days on track to make sure their new car is primarily two things: reliable and fast.

In pre-season testing a team can pull all kinds of tricks to make the outside world believe something that may not be the case. It's a complex time and again relies on the whole team to pull together. One of the aims is not revealing your hand too early to your opponents, who are all around you. Such is the competitive and secretive nature of Formula One that before the 2010 season, Red Bull stuck a graphic of an exhaust on their car, hoping perhaps that a photo taken at high speed will look convincing enough to throw other teams off the scent as to how their exhaust system really works. Most teams now actually employ their own photographer, whose job it is to get tell-tale photos of their opponents' cars in order to try and gain as much information about their rivals as early as possible. These days, with all the high-definition, super-slo-mo camera shots, it's not easy for any team to keep a secret. And any information gleaned will be sent back to base, analysed and acted upon if a team think they've missed a trick.

Another ploy that a team can adopt in pre-season is to run their car almost on petrol fumes and set an impressive time. No one outside the team knows how much fuel they have on board for any particular lap and it'll unnerve the opposition if they suddenly see some incredible and unexpected lap times from a rival team. This has an additional benefit. Sponsors, of course, are key to Formula One because of the astronomical costs involved in the sport. If a team start the season with a sponsor-free car and little interest from potential big-money backers, then some headline-stealing lap times in pre-season can be incredibly useful, not to mention lucrative. Often a potential sponsor will be talking to two or more teams to try and get the right sponsorship package and something like the fastest lap of the day at a pre-season test can prove to be the deciding factor.

On the flip side, if you have a really fast car then you might quickly fill it to the brim with fuel to slow it down, not revealing your hand too early. This is called sandbagging and is another handy tool at the team's disposal. You see, if with weeks to go before the start of the season a team shows they have incredible speed like Brawn did in 2009 or Red Bull in 2011, suddenly they are the focus, the centre of attention. Not only does it raise the bar for the rest of the teams but it also means the quick car is studied, assessed and discussed as others try to work out why it's potentially so fast.

Over the winter, when a car is being tested, the team have no one to compare their progress with. A football manager can see what players the other teams are buying, for example, but in motor racing it's different. The teams will be getting feedback from the CFD programme and the wind tunnel, so they will know where they stand compared to last year or where they wanted to be at any given stage in the season, but they know nothing about their performance relative to their rivals, and that is the essential point. They have zero information on where they are in the pecking order. A car is only fast if all others around it are slower.

For all the above reasons it's fascinating to chat to the team principals and designers on the first few flights of the season. There's always plenty of conjecture, posturing and rumours flying around as the teams fight their corner early on. I've yet to get to the first race having not had a conversation about a car or a revolutionary design element that the other teams are unhappy with. In 2009 they thought the Brawn GP double diffuser was an illegal part until the FIA made clear it was allowed and the rest of the teams quickly went about trying to design their own version as soon as possible.

In 2010 the paddock was awash with speculation about McLaren having brought a revolutionary 'F-duct' to the sport. It essentially meant the driver could use his knee or hand to cover a hole and then blow air through the car to the rear wing, reducing drag and making the car quicker in a straight line. After an appeal about its legality the FIA made it clear the part was legal in their eyes. What followed was a race for the other teams to make their own iteration of an F-duct. After all, if you can't beat 'em, join 'em! It made me laugh actually that most teams, having thought it was an illegal part and spent time and money protesting, then threw thousands, if not millions, at designing their own. It soon became clear, however, that the FIA would ban the 'F-duct' for the following season.

We then had a similar story in 2011 as the teams rounded on Red Bull with questions about a 'flexi-front wing'. The belief in some quarters was that the tips of the front wing were dipping down during the race, making the wing closer to the floor and improving the car's performance. As is usually the way in Formula One, it generated some headlines, plenty of chatter in the pit lane and moans and grumbles from rival team bosses and car designers. I wasn't surprised; it seems if you're the front-running teams this kind of thing is par for the course. Indeed, in 2012 we had it again. This time it was Mercedes who were the ones under scrutiny. I was in the paddock the day before the first race in Albert Park in Australia and one team boss said to me, 'They're up to something and we're not happy about it.' Incredibly, that afternoon it was reported that the same team boss who was so outraged actually already had his engineers designing a similar system in case the part was deemed to be legal! I'm not sure if it's true or not but it's certainly typical F1. Once again the FIA cleared the 2012 Mercedes design, and it was the usual start to a season. Incidentally, that car won the third race of the season after being declared legal, merely increasing the pressure for other teams to follow suit, or at least investigate whether the part was worth having.

The F1 paddock can resemble a school playground in so

many ways. Remember when you were at school and, while you're telling the teacher that your classmate has been naughty and 'dobbing them in' as we called it, you are doing the very same thing? Well, that is F1 all over. In many ways it's indicative of this being an engineering battle as much as a physical, hard-fought racing battle. The race is certainly as much off the track as on it, perhaps even more so. F1 is there to push the envelope and the physical boundaries to make the car go quicker, and that often means pushing the rules to their limit or utilising a loophole – even if that loophole gets swiftly closed.

So once you've designed and tested a car that meets your approval, tested it over the winter and survived any appeals or attempts to derail your impressive new design, it's time for the race weekend to start. Now, even this close to a race start the work never stops; in many cases this can be when it really starts. Before qualifying and the race proper, there are three 'free practice' sessions. They serve multiple purposes. You can do a systems check to make sure everything is working as it should be, try out any new parts to see if they improve the car, give the driver a chance to learn the track, see how your rivals' pace is looking and – possibly most important of all – set up the car for the weekend.

Now you and I buy a car, drive it for five or even twenty years and then sell it. In all that time we don't do a single thing to change the handling or the set-up. In F1 they are constantly changing it. Some of the work they do is down to a driver's own personal specification. Take Michael Schumacher. He likes to have what they call a 'pointy' front end where there is loads of front grip and you get the cars in exactly the right place and in return he doesn't mind the rear moving around a little. At the other end of the scale is Fernando Alonso who throws his car into corners, the front making decisive, sudden jerky movements. However, he is always trusting that the back of the car will grip and keep him on the track.

It's in free practice that the drivers will get their cars ready for a race. After all the simulation work at the factory the team will have a fair idea of how the car will perform and they will have worked to set it up as best they can for their driver. However, if the track is incredibly hot the tyres might overheat; lose grip and the car struggles. The team will then work to solve this by using different compounds or changing the set-up, or by the driver modifying his driving to be easier on the tyres. If the car is struggling to heat its tyres that's an altogether different problem that needs solving and the driver weaving the car, different set-up changes or increasing downforce might help. Downforce is also key to a great race. If you have a circuit with tight corners but long straights, how do you set up? You need lots of downforce in order to stick to the road around the corners, but on the straights this extra downforce creates drag, which slows the car. Then you have to add into the mix the team trying out various new updates that have been provided by the factory, plus assessing how much fuel is needed for the race and how the car performs on high or low fuel.

F1 cars and their drivers are so sensitive that in low-fuel trim the car may be monstrously quick so it's fast in qualifying. However, when it's full with fuel for the race it may handle completely differently and be much slower than the opposition. A car may be able to heat its tyres into the 'operating window' in just one lap so that in qualifying they are immediately up to temperature and the car is again fast in qualifying. However, if the car retains that ability to heat its tyres it may overheat them in the Grand Prix and struggle. This is why testing at a race weekend is so important and why the team are constantly in touch with their driver, tweaking, improving and changing the car all day on a Friday and on a Saturday morning until they have the perfect set-up for the race, all energies focused on trying to get an edge over their rivals.

I actually got in trouble with McLaren at the Malaysian Grand Prix in 2012 when I was given a set of headphones to listen to the team radio. Jenson Button's dad gave them to me, both of us unaware that I shouldn't have been listening in. F1 teams are incredibly secretive, and employ all kinds of people and tools to stop other teams from gaining information that isn't theirs. Eventually I had them taken off me and got a small telling-off. However, what I had heard was fascinating – not only Jenson's initial feedback as he made his way around the Malaysian GP circuit, but also how calm he was behind the wheel, especially considering the numerous tasks he had to carry out such as clutch 'bite point' checks and periods. And when he came in after 15 minutes on track he went through each corner and gave his engineers detailed feedback about how the car performed at every one. They were then able to act upon that information and try to get Jenson the perfect set-up come race day.

There have always been rumours that Rubens Barrichello, who took part in 326 Formula One races, was incredible at setting up a car and that would have been of such good use to his teammates. The set-up of the car is a complex, confusing and largely uncelebrated and unknown part of a driver's job. People say Rubens is legendary at it, feeding back small changes in the car's settings to get it perfectly 'dialled in' to the circuit. It's a great skill Rubens has; however, it isn't just good for him – if his teammate is struggling on the other side of the garage, he can just request to have 'Rubinho's' set-up and it may be perfect.

I'm sure there have been occasions when a driver is frustrated that he has given up his secrets to his teammate, particularly if that teammate then beats him. However, Lewis Hamilton is fascinating on this subject. I was interviewing him in the early part of the 2010 season and we were discussing this very subject. I asked him whether there is genuine trust and sharing of information in the McLaren garage – after all, he and Jenson are racing for McLaren as well as national pride. Lewis's answer reveals just what a natural racer he is. He told me that he'd like every team to know what he has done with his set-up; he'd also like every team to have an identical car – that way, the result of the race comes down to the man who has driven the best, the greatest natural driver, the one who has best coped with the weather, the track and the 200mph battle. He is clearly excited and inspired by the team's technological developments, but I also get the impression that he doesn't want to win a race by having a 'secret set-up' that his teammate hasn't accessed, or by knowing his car is 3 seconds a lap quicker than his rival. Lewis wants raw driving talent to be the determining factor, something that didn't surprise me.

Being compared and assessed against a teammate is a crucial part of an F1 driver's job, but it can also lead at times to tasty rivalries and petty behaviour, to try and gain that all-important edge over an opponent. In motor racing the first person you want to beat is your teammate. We hear stories of teammates keeping each other waiting on purpose, or of those who like to assert their authority by keeping the rest waiting when all the drivers assemble for the pre-race parade.

I've also been told they allegedly play little mind games at every opportunity. After the race when the drivers assemble in the interview area, they may often chat to the state broadcaster of their teammate so that their biggest rival in the same team starts to worry about what is being said back home to their adoring public. So, for example, if you were my teammate and you were French, I could make sure that I went straight to the French media just to faze you or make you question why I was so keen to speak to your fans. It's the small things that can have a big effect and it's understandable as, for a driver, F1 is so unforgiving.

Imagine that in your job, or at your school, there is one colleague or one kid who has *exactly* the same chances, opportunities and equipment as you. And now imagine that it's only the two of you who share such parity, and at the end of each day your performances and achievements are compared directly with the other person, and the results then made public. How hard would that be? I know I'd struggle. As a Formula One driver that is your working day. You drive the car back into the garage and immediately you're presented with a wealth of information about how your teammate compares to you, in great detail. Where you're early on the brakes, late on the throttle, too aggressive with the steering wheel . . . and what the crucial difference in time is between the two. If you're the man on top it must feel wonderful, liberating and confidence-building. How incredibly demoralising, though, if you're the one giving your all but being beaten day after day, race after race.

Well that's just what people thought might happen to Jenson Button when in 2010 he decided to join McLaren. It was a decision that some people simply couldn't fathom. He was joining a team where Lewis was king – he'd been with them since he was a teenager. The sponsors loved him. The engineers loved him. He was still in his early twenties but he'd already delivered a World Championship for McLaren. Yet Jenson backed himself to join up with, and compete with, the set. Remember, there is no hiding place. If you have the same car then the only variable is the driver, and Jenson would have known this when he joined the team. Just as people were wondering if it was the right move for him we all travelled to Australia, race two of that first season with Lewis and he won! The atmosphere when Jenson took that Grand Prix in just his second outing with McLaren almost matched how I remembered the wild abandon of Jenson winning the title. He sprinted into the paddock pursued by snappers, and his dad put on the famous Rocket Red T-shirt – which the team wear when they win a race – live on our show. It felt like his decision had been vindicated, his bravery rewarded . . . and the gauntlet thrown to Lewis. I really felt as he celebrated that it was as much about winning the race as it was about the message it sent to his doubters. The message sent to Lewis and McLaren at that point was also crystal clear – I'm not here to make up the numbers.

A lot is also made of Jenson's ability to make clever decisions when he's under pressure, deal with the tyres well and use his brain as much as his brawn. Another side to him is how realistic and pragmatic he is. I think he'd agree that in raw speed Lewis has an edge, but when you're in the race it's a different story. A few races into his McLaren career and we were at Hungary. Jenson had struggled in qualifying and been knocked out. As I was watching Lewis in the fight for pole position I felt someone grab the back of my pants and lift me skywards. Jenson! He cut me a wry grin and then looked at the timing screen. His face dropped. 'Where does he find that time from?' he asked, then sauntered to his driver room to start the race from eleventh. The following day he finished in the points as Lewis retired.

Drivers are at the summit of an incredibly complicated pyramid. From the silent, methodical design office to loud, frantic workshops all the way up to the top. All that effort lives or dies by the split-second decisions the drivers make behind the wheel. Make the wrong move and millions of pounds and thousands of hours can count for nothing. Martin Brundle has often used the quote, 'Drivers are like light bulbs – when one loses its power you take it out and screw another one in. Simple.' Martin ended his career at Jordan at the end of the 1996 season, and in Monza in 2010 he came out with a cracking line to Eddie Jordan that had us all in stitches but which also demonstrates my point. We were upstairs in Ferrari and we'd been joined by Eddie Irvine, another former Jordan driver. We were talking about EJ making driver decisions and Martin said, 'I'm still waiting for you to tell me I'm not driving for you in 1997, Eddie.' It was said in jest, but we all got the point.

The drivers are the stars, they take the big money, but they are also just employees and in a sport as ruthless as this you have to make tough decisions. I'm sure Martin would have appreciated a phone call back in 1997, but he's gone on to have an amazing second career behind the camera. As an alternative viewpoint, I recall when, in mid-2012, Eddie returned to his former factory, which is now run as the Sahara Force India team and is right on the doorstep of Silverstone. He was talking to Paul di Resta about his plans for 2013, and EJ was clear. He told Paul that if he was still running the team he'd look to move him on to a bigger outfit, and pocket a few quid into the bargain. Eddie's reasoning was that with the speed Paul was showing he'd be too expensive to keep; he'd also be attractive to bigger teams, and Eddie would have taken advantage of that. So, as a driver you are vulnerable if you drive too slowly, and also at risk if you go too fast – which illustrates what an achievement it is to get to the top and stay there. The driver may be the focus of the fans, the darling of the media; exalted when successful, vilified when struggling. He may be a millionaire, a superstar and a hero to millions. However, fail to perform and his exclusive pass to the world of high adrenaline and even higher wages is turned off in an instant.

Sport can bring huge rewards but it can be cruel too. When your time is up, it's over. And publicly over at that. You can't just slow down your workload or be moved to a less demanding part of the business. The job you know, what you've trained for over many years, the very thing that has motivated you, kept you disciplined, given you a sense of purpose – finished at a stroke. I've seen plenty of drivers lose their seats in the short time I've been involved with F1 and there is always a common theme: it hurts. But with so much at stake in F1, there's no time for regrets, no room for sentiment – the king is dead, long live the king. The team has to regroup straightaway, keep looking forward. There may be a new hero, but the dream for any team stays the same. The aim of winning is, and must be, bigger than any one individual.

4

The painful lessons

On lap forty-four of the Canadian Grand Prix, 10 June 2007, Polish driver Robert Kubica was travelling at 190mph, fighting for position, battling his rivals, doing what a racing driver was born to do. As he approached the hairpin at the famous Gilles Villeneuve circuit in good conditions on a dry track, he clipped a car he was passing. In an instant he slid to the right, and on the grass run-off his car was launched into the air, Kubica totally helpless. As he careered forwards, he swiped the barrier, ripping the right front wheel off his car, then the nose started to dip, as he slammed headfirst into the wall that was running along the side of the track.

The impact was ferocious. It ripped a further two wheels off his now disintegrating BMW, so that all that was left was the engine and driver's 'survival cell'. Furthermore, on this occasion even the nosebox came off, leaving his feet vulnerable, but thankfully he didn't go on to hit anything front first. In fact, as he dug into the grass he proceeded to roll over, across the line of cars still racing and came to rest alongside the barrier on the opposite side of the track. His accident happened at full velocity around a circuit famous for delivering incredibly high speeds even by Formula One standards.

Instantly there were marshals racing towards his now still car as commentators, spectators and medics looked for signs of life. Robert had hit the wall at such a speed that he was subjected to a staggering force of 75g. Consider that an emergency stop in a road car is 1g or a hard-braking manoeuvre in a modern F1 car is 5g, and you get some kind of idea about the forces placed upon his body that sunny afternoon in Canada. It was thirteen years since the sport lost Ayrton Senna and Roland Ratzenberger in just one weekend and, as I watched events unfold from the comfort of my living room, I must confess that I feared the worst.

He'd still been travelling at 186mph when he clipped the barrier at a 75-degree angle. The whole accident happened in around 10 seconds. Would he ever race again? After a full examination once he'd been extricated from his car and taken to the medical centre and then on to hospital, it was discovered that his injuries amounted to nothing more than an ankle sprain and light concussion. As for racing again, Robert declared himself 'ready to race' and it was only at the insistence of the sport's governing body that it was decided he would have to miss the next race. He returned to the cockpit just three weeks later and finished fourth.

It's an almost unbelievable story that owes much to the drivers who insisted things changed, the sport's governors who listened to them and, sadly, to those who lost their lives, meaning the subject of safety will never be off the agenda in Formula One. Unfortunately, however, it hasn't always been this way.

One of the most outspoken critics of Formula One safety when he was racing was the three-time world champion Sir Jackie Stewart. It would have taken immense bravery to stand up and say, 'This is my job and I don't expect to die doing it.' Some would have seen it almost as a weakness, admitting you are scared, that the speeds and danger of Formula One are too much for you. But Jackie knew why he was taking on the doubters, of whom there were many, as he had experienced the pain of losing friends and colleagues time and time again, and it was simply too much. Thankfully he enjoyed such respect and had achieved so much that people sat up and took notice – as they needed to.

Sir Jackie drove from 1965 to 1973 and, at that time, if you drove for five years in F1 there was a one-in-three chance you would die. Death was a part of the sport, too much a part of it, as the statistics show: in the 1950s, there were fifteen deaths; in the 1960s, there were twelve; in the 1970s, ten; in the 1980s, four; and in the 1990s there were two. Mercifully, however, there hasn't been a fatality for a Formula One driver since 1994, and that is through no coincidence. In terms of safety, the sport we see today is barely recognisable from that of the fifties, sixties and seventies. Fifty-odd years ago, during a race, you wouldn't slide into a gravel trap or hit an Armco barrier designed to limit the impact. The car wasn't equipped with impact protection or automatic fire extinguishers. In fact, the drivers might not even have been wearing seatbelts. That's right. If you were a racing driver in the 1950s, you'd set off into the race and possibly not even buckle up; the thought of being thrown clear was preferable to being trapped in a burning, mangled car.

While Jackie Stewart did so much for the sport as a respected world champion, equally as important was the contribution of world-renowned neurosurgeon Professor Sid Watkins. Sid may not have had the race wins or the world title, but he did have a love of three things: whisky, fishing and Formula One. He was known in F1 circles simply as Sid or 'Prof' and, although our paths rarely crossed, it gave me great pleasure to hear that he was a big fan of the BBC F1 programme. Sid loved racing, and he did so much to transform the sport from one where death was expected and accepted – where, in the darkest days, drivers would pull each other out of crashed cars and races would continue while a driver was trapped in a burning chasis – to one where fatalities are now only a memory. In the wake of Nikki Lauda's fiery Nurburgring crash and the tragic death of the much-loved Jochen Rindt, Sid met with Bernie Ecclestone in the late 1970s and was invited to become the official F1 doctor. Drivers continued to die on the track in Sid's early time in Formula One, but he worked tirelessly to bring about change and put an end to the loss of lives.

Thankfully, we haven't mourned the passing of a driver in almost twenty years; in fact, in Belgium in September 2012 we witnessed the kind of accident that years ago would likely have seen more than one man killed, when Romain Grosjean squeezed Lewis Hamilton at Spa with catastrophic results. As four cars pinged and bounced off and over each other, so much of the emergency response was down to Sid. The medical car, which for many years he rode in, arrived immediately on the scene; marshals with proper training and up-to-date equipment were also immediately present, while a doctor was straight over to Fernando Alonso to assess his injuries, and the medical helicopter Sid insisted on was waiting to fly a driver to hospital if necessary. Meanwhile, the medical centre was on standby, with state-of-the-art facilities ready to deal with serious trauma.

Formula One owes Professor Sid Watkins so much, and after his passing, aged eighty-four, there was a rare atmosphere during the Singapore race weekend, from the drivers and teams paying their respects on the grid pre-race to the book of remembrance in the paddock. Usually it's the men behind the wheel who are put on the highest pedestal, but that Sunday in Singapore we paid our respects to a man who possessed another, far more vital, impressive and humbling talent – the ability to save lives.

One of my favourite experiences of presenting F1 so far has been spending time with Sir Stirling Moss. He has an amazing house in London, which he bought many moons ago. From the outside you'd have no idea it's home to one of British racing's most famous faces – apart from one thing. Each window has a bit of metalwork in front of it, a kind of 'fake balcony', if you like. And the design of the metalwork? A classic old-school racing car, the kind Stirling enjoyed plenty of success in. When you enter the house, you are faced with an instant memorabilia overload, including an annual that Stirling has made up of all his racing years. The strange thing about the house is that it's quite narrow but very tall, and passing up the middle is a spiral staircase. However, with his love of gadgets and all things technological, Stirling had a lift put in – in fact, it was the lift that was my reason for visiting. Weeks before, he'd called it and stepped in, only to find the lift itself hadn't arrived at the correct floor, and he fell feet first down the shaft, shattering his ankles.

I arrived and made my way upstairs to where Stirling was. Given that he was recuperating, his house was probably the only place we could really do the interview, but I was delighted as I think you can learn a great deal about someone from where they live. Just like him, Stirling's house was welcoming, traditionally British, if a little eccentric – perfect!

He loves watching all the F1 TV shows and greeted me with a cheery, 'Hello, old boy, looking good on the TV, I see.' Considering his injuries and his age – he was eighty at the time – he looked in remarkably fine fettle. He was instantly asking me about the current crop of F1 drivers and passing judgement on who he thought was going to win the world title. Eventually the talk turned to safety in modern Formula One, and his take was fascinating. Bearing in mind that he'd suffered two near-fatal accidents, one of which had caused him to retire, he actually said he was glad he'd raced in an era when it was far more dangerous than it is now. In his words, 'Going round a corner, knowing if you go off you might die, sure made you feel pretty good when you got through it and you hadn't.' Put another way, the buzz, the thrill and the rewards were all heightened because the stakes were so high.

I asked him what kind of safety devices he'd had in his day, and he scoffed at me before suddenly hauling himself out of his chair. His ever-loving and loyal wife Suzie heard him and shouted down to him, 'The doctor says you're not to walk on those ankles yet!', at which point he flashed me a wicked grin and asked me to follow him.

We headed up to his bedroom, where he asked me to fetch his race bag down from the cupboard, and he got out his race suit and helmet to show me. These days the drivers wear a flame-resistant Nomex suit, which can survive temperatures of 840°C for up to 11 seconds. Stirling's was made out of cotton. Then he told me he'd often drive in a white cotton T-shirt because it was a little cooler. Next, we looked at his helmet. Because he was still racing in classic car races and wanted to do so in the traditional style, the only way he really knew, he was given special dispensation from the racing bodies to use his classic race suit, not drive with a fire extinguisher attached, and to still wear his little leather and cork helmet. Leather and cork?! What use would that be in a high-speed accident? Nowadays, before a current F1 helmet is passed as safe to be raced it is subjected to an 800°C flame for 45 seconds, during which time the heat inside the helmet must not exceed 70°C. Furthermore, the visor has projectiles fired at it at around 300mph and if any of these make dents deeper than 2.5mm, the helmet fails. There are numerous other tests for the current helmets, but those two are a clear example of just what has changed in the last fifty years. The days are no more when Stirling and his pals would drive what the legendary F1 commentator Murray Walker once described as 'mobile death traps'.

What really brought the changes home to me, however, were Sir Stirling's two steering wheels. They hang from hooks on his study wall and are inscribed with the dates and locations of two of his biggest accidents. There is something about them both that takes your breath away: in the middle of each thick metal wheel is a huge dent where Stirling's head, with only a cork hat for protection, made impact. One is from a crash in 1960 in Spa-Francorchamps, the famous Belgian track, and came during a black weekend for Formula One. At 140mph, the rear wheel came off Stirling's Lotus. Still travelling at 90mph, he hit a bank and was thrown from the car, breaking both his legs. The following day both Chris Bristow, a garage owner's 22-year-old son from London, and 26-year-old British driver Alan Stacey, in just his seventh race, lost their lives at the same corner. The long, sweeping Burnenville had bitten back that weekend. That same race saw Michael Taylor crash his Lotus 18; he too was thrown from the car, apparently taking out a tree with his body and suffering several broken bones. Yet despite the tragedy, and the injuries, Stirling returned to racing that very season, winning the US Grand Prix. It seemed, sadly, that dying was as much a part of the sport as winning in those days. It certainly didn't put people off.

Stirling's top-class career ended just two years later, in 1962, when he crashed at Goodwood, on the south coast of England, and was in a coma for a month.

There is simply no doubt that Stirling Moss is alive today not because of the brilliant safety of his racing car or the attention paid to keeping drivers alive in his day, but because of extraordinary good fortune and the fact he's not the kind of guy ever to stop fighting, either on the track or off it. Sadly, other drivers over the years haven't been as lucky as Stirling was.

I often find it strange when we visit classic F1 circuits to think of the sadness that was once so common at those places. In 2011, I was filming with David Coulthard on the track at Monza. We were making an opening piece for that weekend's programme and the two of us were delivering lines to the camera just at the entrance to the Parabolica. I went for a walk as David's filming was due to take 15 minutes or so, when suddenly it dawned on me as I stood by the barrier looking over at the spectator area that this was the scene of one of the darkest ever moments for Formula One and its safety record.

In 1961, Wolfgang von Trips was a German Ferrari driver who was having the season of his life. He arrived at the Italian track needing only to finish third to be crowned world champion. He started the race on pole and had so far had the perfect weekend, but it would end in tragedy. He was racing Scotland's Jim Clark around the famous old Monza circuit and they were on lap two when disaster struck. Suddenly the German driver's rear wheels collided with the Scot's front left wheel. Von Trips slid on to the grass, up a steep spectator banking and into the crowd. He was thrown fatally from the car and his Ferrari somersaulted into the spectators, killing fifteen people. The most astonishing thing of all, perhaps the one thing that gives us the greatest insight into the approach to safety in that era, was that the race wasn't even halted; they continued for a further forty laps as the dead were carried off and the injured were treated.

This was the last ever race on the old banking at Monza – after that crash the ten-kilometre circuit was reconfigured to the track they use today. However, the old banking remains, a relic of an era in racing that is thankfully in the distant past. I often head to the old part of the track when I'm in Italy. It's extremely atmospheric – a huge, wide, steep piece of banked track that is slowly starting to show its age. Hopefully it remains forever as a reminder of how far we've come in terms of safety.

A less dramatic but equally poignant memorial to one of the sport's darkest moments, and its greatest drivers, sits in a quiet forest on the edge of Germany's Hockenheim F1 circuit, and is the spot where Jim Clark lost his life, seven years after Wolfgang von Trips. In 2010 I was at Hockenheim presenting that year's German Grand Prix, and I felt compelled to pay my respects as, for the first time in my life, I was at the very same circuit where Jim lost his life forty-two years earlier. Part of the magic of Jimmy was his record – at the time of his death he'd achieved more wins and pole positions than any other driver, and he's been placed at the top of many 'greatest driver' lists over the years. He is my racing hero, and so on a damp, cold and windy German evening I decided that I wanted to go to the place where Jimmy had passed away.

Hockenheim is one of the most famous and historic tracks in the world, but in 1968 it was a dangerous high-speed circuit that was double the length it is today. The circuit organisers have erected a shrine to Jim Clark on a footpath leading away from the track, but the spot where he actually crashed is really rather well hidden. I wasn't interested in the modern memorial, that wasn't enough for me. With the weather closing in, however, trekking around in the forest looking for a wooden cross a few inches high was becoming something of a needle-in-a-haystack quest. After walking for the best part of 30 minutes myself, the producer Sarah and cameraman Matt started asking passersby. To our surprise, nobody could tell us where the small, understated shrine actually was and everyone directed us to the modern memorial, which I knew was nowhere near the old track. Undeterred, we followed our noses and were eventually rewarded. Pushing past some tall, old trees into the dense forest, I looked to my left and saw, disappearing off into the distance, a clear, low line of much younger trees, about a track's width wide and flanked by huge great pines – the very same trees that would have been there when Jim was racing. We had found the now disused old track, long ripped up.

It was quite a strange experience to see nature slowly taking back what was rightfully hers, but also knowing that for the best part of half a century the very spot I was standing on was asphalt and alive with the sound of the world's greatest racing cars. We made our way a little further on and just to the left of the circuit, before a small bank that leads to a gentle stream, there it was. Hidden beneath a tall pine tree stood a very simple wooden cross with Jim's face on it, and growing nearby was a Scottish thistle. I am unsure if a fan planted the thistle, but I like to think they didn't.

The ironic thing about Jim Clark's death was that he was actually racing in a relatively insignificant Formula Two race – this was in the days when drivers would compete in all kinds of formulae all year round. In fact, he was actually due to be driving at Brands Hatch that day but chose to be in Germany instead. On the fifth lap of his heat, Jim's car veered off the track and crashed into the trees. In his day there was no such thing as an Armco or Tecpro barrier to help keep him safe or a crash survival cell which today's racers have. As Jackie Stewart says, 'Have a crash in those days and you were likely to hit a wall, a telegraph pole, or even a house.' Well, the forest itself was Jim's crash barrier that afternoon. There has never been an official answer as to why he crashed; however, many have speculated that he was grappling with a deflating tyre or perhaps had an issue with the engine. Whatever the cause, the racing community was sure it wasn't driver error, such was Jim's natural ability behind the wheel. Regardless of the facts surrounding Jim Clark's untimely death, his legacy very much lives on. For weeks after Jim's death, it was ordered that all Lotus road cars carry a black nose badge as a sign of respect. I have one sitting in my study.

The heavens then opened and, soaked to the skin, we headed back to our hotel, past the guesthouse where Jim had stayed the weekend he died, and raised a stein of beer or two that night to the memory of Jim Clark.

Having lost far, far too many drivers in the 1950s, 60s and 70s, it became clear that it was time to do something. Jackie Stewart was the first to really take a stand, and I'm pleased to say that in the decades that have followed, drivers have felt much more empowered to speak out when they don't think something is safe. Things began to change for the better and, looking back now, it seems amazing that it took so long for the sport to make the changes that today we take for granted.

In 1968 the FIA brought in the rule that the roll bar must be higher than a driver's head. Even today we see evidence of legislation saving lives. In 2010 I was in the Red Bull hospitality suite in Valencia, watching the European Grand Prix unfold, with Eddie Jordan to my right and David Coulthard just behind me. It had been an incredibly hot day and I was grateful for the chance to relax during the race. Suddenly there was a loud gasp from the crowded room. I'd been looking at my phone, but as I glanced at the screen Mark Webber was high in the air and coming down at speed. In all honesty, at that moment I feared the worst. It worried me too that David had instinctively grabbed my shoulders from behind – a reaction like that from a man who had raced and crashed F1 cars told me that this was a bad one.

Mark had caught the back wheel of Heikki Kovalainen's Lotus as he tried an overtake, and as the tip of the Red Bull's nose caught the fast-spinning rear wheel of Kovalainen's car it was flipped through the air, wiping out an advertising hoarding that was ten feet above the track before landing upside down and sliding into the barriers. I immediately went into TV mode and worked out what we'd do in such a circumstance. However, within just a second of the car coming to a stop Mark had already removed his steering wheel and it was clear he was okay. Forty-two years earlier they had stipulated roll bars above a driver's head and here it was having probably just saved a life. That evening the Red Bull guys let me into the garage to have a look at what remained of the chassis, and I was blown away by how intact it was. The front crash structure had done its job – there was a little damage to the left side pod, and that was pretty much it. The team did reveal to me that one of the pedals was damaged . . . and the total of Mark's injuries? A bruised toe. Everyone around us agreed that just a few years earlier that crash would have most likely been fatal.

In 1970 the new double guardrail was introduced to stop cars going under the barrier; spectators were moved a minimum of three metres from the track and, not surprisingly, straw bales were banned. Considering they were highly flammable and F1 cars were at one time very prone to catching fire, it seems a wild idea now to use straw bales as crash barriers, but they were standard 'protection' for many years.

In the 1980s and 90s, the new rules started to really make a difference: the driver's survival cell had to extend in front of their feet, which couldn't be further forward than the front axle; the cars were being subjected to ever more stringent tests; and in 1984 the FIA stipulated that a driver had to carry a 'Superlicence' in order to take part in Formula One. An FIA Superlicence exists to make sure those competing at the very top of the sport have the necessary skills and experience to handle Formula One racing. For you or I to get one we'd need a Grade A competition licence, and then to become champion in a lower category of motorsport than F1, such as Formula Two or GP2, or even IndyCar in the USA.

Alternatively, consistently strong race finishes in those categories can result in a Superlicence being awarded. Effectively, show your competency and achievements and a Superlicence can be yours. Mind you, it's not cheap. It's been reported that in 2010 Lewis Hamilton paid almost £250,000 for his Superlicence, because in addition to the cost of the licence itself, drivers have to pay an extra sum for each point they score in Formula One. When you think there are twenty-five points for a win, you can see how the costs soon escalate. But if you want to race in F1 you have to have a Superlicence.

I would imagine that by 1994, the F1 community was feeling pretty confident, having not lost a driver in a race or in qualifying since 1982. However, that twelve-year streak was about to end in terrible fashion.

For most racing fans in their thirties, Ayrton Senna was seen as the master of F1. It's hard to describe now to people who never saw him race just how sensational he was to watch. His car would twitch and slide around even when he was going in a straight line. He was engaged in a constant battle for grip on a race track, and he did so with a swagger and a style that resonated with me in my early teens. I'll never forget the weekend when even the advances in safety that F1 had seen by the mid-1990s weren't enough to save his life, or that of the Austrian driver Roland Ratzenberger the day before.

It frustrates me greatly when I hear people talk only of Ayrton that weekend. Ratzenberger must also never be forgotten, as his death helped bring about one of the greatest modern driver safety devices. He was a year younger than the great Brazilian, and had a career that was largely spent in sports car racing, coming fifth in the 1993 Le Mans race. Eventually he saw his dream realised in 1994 when he signed a short-term deal to drive in five races for the Simtek team run by Nick Wirth. In race one he failed to qualify; then in the following race in Japan he had a creditable eleventh-place finish, having started twenty-sixth and last on the grid. Little was he to know that it would be his last ever motor race.

Two weeks later, in qualifying for the San Marino Grand Prix at Imola, it's believed that Roland Ratzenberger ran wide and damaged his car's front wing. Rather than pit, as he was once again chasing the final grid spot, he continued to push. Along the back straight, at high speed and under increased loads, the wing is alleged to have finally failed, causing him to crash into the outside wall at around 195mph. The cause of death was a basilar skull fracture – a fracture at the very base of the skull. The sport was in mourning for Roland. It had been a big shock for all involved, coming as it did a day after a large crash for Rubens Barrichello, the Brazilian driver competing for Jordan who became airborne on a high kerb at the final chicane and broke his arm and nose. Sadly, as we're now only too well aware, that wasn't the end of the trauma that weekend.

Senna was distraught at the death of the rookie driver from Austria. It is said that he commandeered a track marshal to take him to the site of Ratzenberger's accident, before he made his way to the medical centre to get information about the health of his colleague. The news wasn't good, but it was decided that the race would go on, though not before the drivers got together to discuss re-forming the Grand Prix Drivers' Association. Senna was instrumental in pushing the idea and spent his final morning meeting fellow drivers to discuss re-establishing the group, which had disbanded in 1982 after twenty years, reportedly due to the effects of changing commercial arrangements in the sport. It was an unstable time. Ironically, Senna was set to lead the GPDA from the next race in Monaco, but it was a race he was never to take part in.

On race day the bad news kept coming. An accident on the start line sent a tyre into the crowd, injuring fans, and led to the cars following a safety car for the next few laps. These days the safety car is a modern, high-performance sports car, driven to the very limit by an experienced professional racing driver. Back in 1994, the safety car was a sporty version of the family car, the Vauxhall Vectra. The problem with a safety car not carrying high speeds is that it allows the F1 cars behind it to lose tyre pressure and heat, both of which lead to a dramatic change in the cars' handling.

Eventually the race restarted and on lap six, Senna, the triple world champion, immediately set a quick pace, followed by Michael Schumacher in his Benetton. As Senna entered the high-speed Tamburello corner on lap seven, the car left the track and struck a concrete wall, and the man believed by many to be the greatest racing driver there has ever been was killed. My abiding memory of that weekend is the news bulletin, the moment when Moira Stewart broke the news to the nation: 'Good evening. The former world motor racing champion, Ayrton Senna, has been pronounced clinically dead after a crash at this afternoon's San Marino Grand Prix. Senna suffered serious head injuries when his car left the track and crashed into a concrete wall.' I remember even then thinking she must be mistaken, that Senna would pull through. He wouldn't, and Formula One left that weekend having lost two drivers in just two days.

The words of Michael Schumacher were spot on in the post-race press conference. He had won the Grand Prix, but all thoughts were with the drivers who had lost their lives as Michael said, 'Let's hope we learn from this, I think there is a lot to learn from. Things like this shouldn't happen without taking the experience from it.' And that is exactly what the sport did.

Even without Ayrton to lead them, the drivers did re-form the Grand Prix Drivers' Association, which to this day makes a real difference to the safety of the sport. There is a genuine understanding in Formula One that the drivers can help to give a really accurate idea of how safe things are and what can be changed to make things safer. They are regularly listened to and consulted by the FIA; after all, they're the ones who have to sit behind the wheel. The driver who took over the Williams seat from Senna was my good friend David Coulthard, and he was instrumental in raising the sides of the cockpit as a result of his own experiences. He'd had a big accident in 2008 in Melbourne, when he hit Alexander Wurz, the BMW driver, and rode up on to Wurz's car, narrowly missing the Austrian driver's head. David argued that the cockpit sides should be higher to prevent similar accidents, and they were subsequently raised. Who knows what injuries have been prevented as a result.

To this day, the drivers meet at each and every Grand Prix to discuss all kinds of matters, with driver safety always on the agenda. Sometimes they consider big issues; on other occasions they talk about the smaller things, such as kerb heights or advertising hoardings. That's right – advertising hoardings! David told me that in Monaco a few years ago, the drivers complained that a huge advert just after the Loews hairpin was distracting them. It was a huge picture of a very beautiful lady, and the drivers complained that she was distracting them as they drove an F1 car around one of the most complicated and unforgiving circuits on the F1 calendar! Some things never change.

However, the drivers these days are incredibly aware not only of the onus on them to speak out about safety, but also of the fact that the FIA will take them seriously. In 2011 it was the first time F1 had ever raced in India, and I took Jenson Button on a tour around the track in an auto-rickshaw. It was only a bit of fun for TV, but also a really interesting eye-opener for me to spend time with a driver who was getting his first look at a new track. Of course, his prime concern was to look for the braking zones and the perfect turn-in points, but he was very clear and open about any safety issues that he spotted. At one point we came around a left-hander and he immediately said, 'Well, that needs to change – I'll speak to Charlie.' Charlie Whiting is the race director, and he walks the track to inspect it at every race. It seemed that one thing might have escaped the officials' attention, but Jenson was straight on to it. As the track went left, I followed it with my eyes and couldn't see any problem. It was only when Jenson pointed out the barrier across the grass, quite a way from us, that I realised what he meant. He was concerned that the angle of the barrier made it possible for someone to have a head-on crash, and was keen for there to be some kind of protection – such as tyres – put in the way.

Now this is clearly more serious than hitting a barrier at an angle and was a good spot by him. It was at this point that I realised the knowledge a driver has is invaluable in such a situation. I guess I thought that twenty feet of grass was enough to stop, or turn the car. He knew, through experience, just how much ground an F1 car covers in a short space of time, and was happy to use that knowledge to make the track safer.

Driver input through the GPDA was one great thing to come out of that terrible weekend in Imola. Another was the HANS – Head and Neck Support – device, which is nowadays compulsory in most forms of motor racing, to prevent the very injury that took the life of Roland Ratzenberger. Made of carbon fibre and U-shaped, it sits over the driver's chest and around his neck, with small tethers connecting it to the helmet. The seatbelts then pass over the HANS device, strapping it to the driver's body. Therefore, in the event of an accident, the HANS will stop the driver's head from being thrown forwards. After 1994, F1 showed interest in the equipment and it became mandatory from 2003 onwards – a further development that may have saved many lives over the years.

The other most significant safety advancement in F1 is the driver's survival cell. Go back to the dark days, and an F1 car was usually just lightweight panels bolted to a tubular chassis. Fuel sloshed around in an unprotected tank, and the cars often caught fire in an accident. In today's models, the survival cell extends from in front of the driver's feet back to where the engine is bolted on to the chassis. Effectively, everything is designed to be attached to the car, and also to disintegrate or be ripped off in an accident. Not only does this leave the driver in the centre of a safe, carbon-fibre shell, but the parts that get broken off help to dissipate the energy. That is why an F1 accident often looks so spectacular, with bits flying everywhere – it is by design.

The car itself is made up of layer upon layer of carbon-fibre sheets, each about as thick as one-fifth of a human hair. The sheets are layered on top of each other until they are 6mm thick and incredibly strong. The teams, in conjunction with the FIA, then subject this 'shell' to multiple examinations, including an impact test, a static load test and a lateral strength test – all designed to see how the car would react in various different types of accident. Kevlar, the same material as is used in bulletproof vests, is employed in F1 cars to provide a different type of protection. Imagine if a car part falls on to the track in front of you. Even if it isn't moving that piece of debris will still create a significant impact if your car is doing 200mph, and the Kevlar is designed to protect against projectiles hitting the car's side. As well as this, there is an accident data recording system in all cars, so that if there is a crash the first medic on the scene can use the information to gain an idea of the severity of the impact. The driver is held in place with a six-point harness that is released with just one movement and requires only one hand to operate it. A driver must prove he can exit the car in an emergency in just 5 seconds. To aid his release, the steering wheel can be removed instantly.

Despite all these safety measures, accidents will still happen. One of the drivers I've really enjoyed working with is the Mexican flyer Sergio Perez. He is a great young racing driver, full of enthusiasm and energy and not short on talent either. In Monaco in 2011, however, he had one of the biggest crashes in my recent F1 memory. As he exited the famous Monaco tunnel, he lost control of the car under braking, hit the barrier and slid sideways at high speed into it. The stop was almost instantaneous and the impact severe. What helped save him that day weren't just the advances in car safety, but also the fact that the circuits themselves are much safer than ever before. He collided with a new type of barrier called a Tecpro barrier – if there had only been tyres or, as it was years ago, just metal Armco, the crash would have been far more serious. These barriers had been through five years of extensive testing and were designed especially with F1 in mind. They don't collapse on impact, they absorb huge amounts of energy, reduce the power of the g-force and, even at speeds of 220kph in testing, the cars never rode over the top of them. Sergio Perez has since said that his accident left him feeling ill for about five races, and he missed one race. Seventeen years earlier, Karl Wendlinger crashed in exactly the same place and spent weeks in a coma – clear evidence that the changes are working.

Of course Formula One will never be a totally safe sport, and it's dangerous to think that we will never again see a fatality at a Formula One event. The quest for a safer sport will never stop, and there are regular reminders that it mustn't. I simply can't imagine how I would react if I was in a position where I had to break the news to the viewing public that a driver had crashed and died. The closest I have come to how that must feel was in 2009 when the Brazilian driver Felipe Massa suffered a huge blow on the head during qualifying for the Hungarian Grand Prix. He was following his fellow Brazilian, Rubens Barrichello, when he just went straight on at turn four. No one could quite work out what had happened at the time, but it eventually became clear that a spring had come loose from the Brawn GP car in front of Felipe and, as he approached the bouncing piece of metal, it struck his helmet above the left eye, the force of the impact fracturing his skull. Medics were immediately on the scene, he was airlifted to hospital and, despite initially being described as in a life-threatening condition, he made a swift and full recovery. He didn't drive again that season, but after extensive tests by the FIA he returned the following year.

It was an intense experience for me, and a steep learning curve. People often assume you have lots of information coming to you from the television gallery that you're holding back, but in fact we were as much in the dark as the audience at home. We didn't want to replay the accident on screen in case it proved to be more serious, so there was no way of us analysing the footage and reporting back. My overriding emotion on air, I remember, was one of disbelief: I couldn't take in that we were discussing a serious injury to a driver. It is so rare now and not something that I'd considered I'd ever need cover, but that just goes to show how quickly our perception of whether a sport is dangerous or not can change.

I found the atmosphere interesting the following day. The sport knew Felipe was out of grave danger and thoughts returned very quickly to the racing – the world of F1 has learned not to dwell on the past. As I went for my traditional Saturday-night run I stopped where Felipe's tyre marks went straight into the wall. TV didn't do justice to the speed at which he was travelling, the distance he covered or the forces with which he hit the tyres. I understood much more at that moment, and I'll never forget it.

Surviving high-speed accidents is not a new phenomenon, though. It might come as a surprise to learn that the highest g-rating on record suffered by any racing driver is believed to have been experienced by David Purley in 1977. The British driver was pushing his LEC Formula One car to the limit as he made his way through the Becketts corner at Silverstone. (It was early in the race weekend and he was taking part in pre-qualifying. In those days, there used to be such a large number of entrants that they had to whittle down the field before qualifying actually started.) Mid-corner, the throttle on the car is believed to have jammed, sending him towards the barriers at 140mph. It was estimated that he hit the barriers at 108mph and decelerated to 0mph in just twenty-six inches. He didn't walk away unscathed: his heart stopped six times, he suffered twenty-nine bone fractures and ended up with one leg two inches shorter than the other. However, he did return to racing and the record still stands: on that day in 1977, David Purley survived the unimaginable force on his body of 179.8g.

Since the dark days of the fifties and sixties, the sport, its drivers and governing body have made it their priority to mini-mise the risks and increase safety. But can you ever completely remove the dangers of 200mph, open-cockpit racing? Of course you can't – but that should never stop us from trying.

5

The commercialisation
of Formula One

In 2012, at the very start of the season in Australia, I was chatting to the press officer for one of the oldest and most respected names in Formula One. We were sitting outside having a coffee a day before the cars took to the track for the first time that year. We were discussing how the team's winter preparations had gone, and I asked the PR person what the team's target was for the season. The reply staggered me: 'Well, we've got the funds in place to make the end of the year.' I could barely believe that, in a sport where the smallest updates cost thousands, and millions of people watch the races, here was one of the established teams stating that having enough money to survive the season was an achievement. If it hadn't come from a member of the team itself, I would have dismissed it as a wild rumour. It's a regular occurrence, after all, for gossip about the financial turmoil of smaller teams to spread like wildfire, so I take most talk of this nature with a large pinch of salt – after all, as my day unfolded, I was told that another team towards the back of the grid were in dire financial trouble. It was claimed that they didn't need to pay a large chunk of money to the promoter until after the fourth race, at which point they'd fold and disappear from the grid, but at the time of writing (halfway through the year) they're still racing.

However, there is no doubt that since the financial crisis of 2008/09 the excesses of the late nineties are a thing of the past and, who knows, perhaps the sport will never experience again those heady days.

What took Formula One into the financial stratosphere was the interest from tobacco manufacturers, which started back in the 1960s. Many people think the cigarette brands only got involved in the eighties, but the very first car to carry commercial cigarette sponsorship was, unsurprisingly, the groundbreaking Lotus team. Always looking for a way to get ahead of the rest of the pack, the team advertised Gold Leaf in 1968 at the Monaco Grand Prix, and after Graham Hill took pole position and the win, perhaps it was inevitable that others would follow suit.

Four years later Philip Morris got involved, and things really started to ramp up as the cars became iconic, with the sponsor an integral part of the look. I remember with real fondness the Black JPS Lotus car, Williams being sponsored by Rothmans and Marlboro plastered all over the Ferrari. All successful cars, all race or championship winners, and all helped a great deal by the money tobacco brought with it.

It seemed a match made in heaven: in return for lavish press and PR events, free cigarettes handed out at races and models employed by the tobacco firms to sex up the race weekends, the tobacco companies got unrivalled global exposure. They pumped hundreds of millions of pounds a season into the sport, a tap that still hasn't been turned off: even today the official name of the Ferrari team is Scuderia Ferrari Marlboro – the same partnership that has been in existence since the eighties, even though tobacco sponsorship was banned in 2006.

The ban on cigarette advertising in the sport forced teams to look for new ways to fund themselves, and in recent years we've seen an influx of big-name car brands deciding that Formula One is the ultimate way to sell their road cars to the public. The likes of Honda, Toyota and BMW – global brands boasting turnover of millions, if not billions of pounds – arrived. Naturally, these companies have to make a splash, so they have grand hospitality units in the paddock; they need success, so they pump hundreds of millions of pounds into car research and development, and furnish armies of PR personnel with press releases and juicy media trips.

But none of that guarantees success, of course. Toyota were rumoured to be the biggest spenders of all, with estimates being bandied around the paddock of a half-a-billion-pound budget per season. They lasted for eight years, employing big-name drivers such as Jarno Trulli and Ralf Schumacher. For all their time and trouble, they exited in 2009, having not scored a podium in four of those eight seasons nor having picked up a single victory, with a fourth-place finish in the constructors' battle the best they could have hoped for. Having run a team in the 1960s and supplied engines to many successful teams, Honda rejoined in 2006 and stayed only for three seasons. Jenson Button and Rubens Barrichello drove for them and in those three seasons they managed just three podiums. And what of BMW, the German manufacturer who had again enjoyed success as an engine supplier but now wanted to race in their own right? They lasted just four years, also exiting in 2009, with just one win to show for their effort. So what happened in those few years for the car companies to decide to walk away? As we all now know, they were hit by the global downturn and decided F1 was not in their 'recession-busting' plans.

And this is where it gets interesting. Big manufacturers will enter the sport when it suits them, spend the money they need to gain success, which in turn clearly increases the amount other teams need to spend to compete with them, and when F1 no longer fits into their plans they can simply walk away. Look at the archetypal privateer team, Williams. They exist solely to race; they don't have the option of walking away and pursuing other interests when things get tough, because for them there is nothing else. In many ways they are left to pick up the pieces when other teams come and go.

Eddie Jordan often gets exasperated with the performance of the smaller teams in Formula One. He finds it hard to fathom how, after being involved in the sport for a few seasons and having spent astronomical sums, perhaps as much as £70 million, the likes of Caterham, Marussia and HRT haven't come close to scoring a point. In some ways I can relate to his sense of frustration.

EJ entered Formula One in 1991 – in his fifth race in Canada he had a fourth- and fifth-place finish, and his first podium in Japan in 1994. Even though in his day you only got points for finishing in the top six places on the track, Eddie's team still managed to do so in their first season. Contrast that to the Marussia or Caterham F1 teams. They entered the sport in 2010, taking the number of teams involved up to twelve. At the time the points were handed out to the first ten finishers, yet midway through the 2012 season, despite decent budgets, neither team had managed to get that coveted points finish.

So how was EJ able to do what other, more recent teams haven't managed? Many believe it's due to the progression of the sport, the fact that the huge finances involved have raised the stakes, the professionalism and the levels required to achieve success. Whether it's the financial investment of the cigarette companies that set the bar, or the influx over the years of big-spending car manufacturers, the result is a sport where it's incredibly difficult to start from scratch and become a force to be reckoned with. It's now so much more expensive to be successful than it was a decade or so ago; quite simply, it's now a case of 'How fast can you afford to go?', as they say in F1.

Although Williams and McLaren have been around for many years, they became established in an era when perhaps it was easier to mix it with the big boys and win. When EJ entered Formula One and then almost won the World Championship in 1999, it was already becoming an obscenely expensive sport if you wanted to do it successfully. Now it's perhaps impossible without serious megabucks. Imagine if you fancied getting involved now. You'd first of all look at the lack of success of recent start-ups, then the wealth Red Bull owner Dietrich Mateschitz boasts, the power of Ferrari and the sponsors needed to support McLaren – after that, you'd take a big gulp before jumping in feet first! Eddie got in, set up a privateer team, won races, created headlines and then got out. And along the way he probably had more fun in a day than most people allow themselves across a whole F1 career.

The Jordan team were loved for their 'rock 'n' roll' values and little has changed today – EJ plays with his band on most evenings in various bars and campsites until the wee small hours. (Despite being in his sixties, Eddie has a band that pretty much travels the world with us, gigging in various bars and clubs in the cities Formula One visits. He's our very own rock 'n' roll star!) It's also apparent where that madness that Jordan GP embodied originated. Our first day together as a new presenting team was at Dunsfold, at the *Top Gear* test track, when five of us set times in the 'reasonably priced car' for the *Top Gear* magazine. Well, I say five – it was actually only four, as Eddie decided his chosen tactic was to make sure the handbrake was ruined for everyone else. Cue wheelspins, handbrake turns, across the grass, over the line backwards . . . and a bunch of *Top Gear* people looking rather forlornly at a smoking family saloon. Not that EJ gave two hoots; to him it was just like every other day – there was fun to be had and mischief to be made!

Many people don't even know that Eddie was a decent racing driver in his day, winning races and titles, eventually competing in British Formula Three, a serious race series where young hopefuls prepare themselves for a career in F1. However, he had a bad crash in 1976 in which he broke both his ankles and, despite racing on until 1979, EJ had clearly decided that he would be better off on the pit wall and in the boardroom rather than behind the wheel. Not that stopping racing slowed him down in any way – I'm reliably informed that even as a boss Eddie still did everything at 200mph!

While it's clear that the money that has been pumped into F1 may have led to raised standards of competitiveness and professionalism, I think it's also been good news for the fans watching at home. As the increased costs have generally been covered by bringing on board more sponsors, it has obliged teams to find unique ways to service them, and that includes getting them in front of the TV cameras. Big-spending and generous sponsors are now part of the fabric of the sport – F1 would find it hard to survive without them. What do they get in return for their cash? Time on the TV! Imagine F1 without any TV stations covering it – I believe it wouldn't be written about in the papers, the grandstands wouldn't be filled, the big-name sponsors would disappear and the drivers would all be earning pennies. TV is the heartbeat of the sport. For this reason our requests for access are usually accepted pretty readily.

David Coulthard told me that there is no doubt most drivers dislike having to spend hours talking to the media, but they also realise how important it is. You can understand that if you've just won your first ever Grand Prix, all you really want to do is ring your parents or go and give your engineers a celebratory embrace – but that just isn't an option for a race winner in Formula One. Their first commitment is to the media, and the sport's guidelines stipulate that they must speak to the press. The sport's governing body clearly understands the importance of making sure the teams and the drivers fulfil their media obligations. Therefore after each session, from free practice until the race itself, the driver is required to go into the 'pen', which is where they are paraded around by their press officer and offered to any TV outlet that wants to speak to them. It's a small area in the paddock, a square of crush barriers with the reporters and TV cameras on the outside, drivers in the middle – it actually reminds me a bit of when I'd go to the cattle market as a young lad in

Norfolk! Even during the race, each team must put forward a designated person who will speak to the media and answer questions about what is happening as the Grand Prix unfolds.

I guess these arrangements actually work for both sides. It means the TV crews get a guaranteed interview with one of the stars of the sport, and the teams know they can bat away any additional requests for interviews by saying, 'You can have them in the pen.' However, drivers who finish on the podium face a real scrum: first of all, they are ushered to what is known as the 'unilateral' interview, where one person will ask a few questions in English for all the TV channels to transmit if they wish; then they are guided into the global media press conference. This is usually in a small room near the media centre and a select group of the world's press will gather and discuss the race with the podium finishers.

Then the team's press officer will herd the drivers down to the media 'pen'. However, instead of farmers parading their bulls in front of prospective buyers, here you have press officers leading their driver from interview to interview. Finally, usually about an hour after the race has finished, the drivers leave the pen and it is totally up to them whether they carry out any additional media engagements.

I've lost count of the hours I've spent loitering in the paddock, waiting for a driver, only to see them sprint past, head down, shades on, and you know they don't want to talk. I've also been blown out and ignored by drivers on more than one occasion, which is something of a hazard of the job. On the whole, though, the access we get in F1 is impressive, especially compared with other sports I've covered.

Sponsors pay huge sums to be associated with the sport, and the exposure they get from reaching the 100,000 people in the grandstands isn't enough – it's all about TV, and the teams certainly appreciate that. I've spoken to a few drivers over the years who have grumbled about the amount of media they are expected to do, but at the same time they understand that without the hundreds of millions of fans watching at home, they wouldn't be the well-paid stars they are. However, I do feel some sympathy when I am interviewing a driver and a quick look to my left reveals four or five other crews all lining up to do the same thing . . .

People often tweet me or complain on message boards that there are certain 'big-time' drivers that we rarely talk to. In our defence, we put in the requests and it's the same old faces that will turn us down time and time again. It's a fact of life that when you only have a very select group of top drivers who are fighting for wins and titles, demand will always outstrip supply.

However, to get the big interviews it really helps to have on board two people who were on the 'other side of the fence' for so many years. David certainly disarms the drivers, as they still see him predominantly as a mate rather than a journalist – and I think they always will. Not only has David shared a track with those guys and trusted them at 200mph, they've also trusted him, which gives rise to huge mutual respect. The drivers meet with each other, party with each other and often travel with each other; they are members of an exclusive club, who have all made it to the very top of their game. As for Eddie, only someone who has run a team could really get away with the kind of antics he gets up to. From waltzing from motorhome to motorhome as if he runs the team to grabbing even the most respected F1 figures and not letting them go until they give us an interview, he seems to have no shame. Yet, despite his shenanigans, I've never seen anyone get angry with him; they usually just shrug and say, 'That's Eddie!'

Having said all that, I do remember seeing David get angry when one of the people he used to work with refused to tell him something because he was 'now a journalist', which really got DC's back up. There will always be an element of mistrust between the teams and the media because it's a sport that revolves around such intense secrecy. The job of an F1 journalist isn't simply to report the results of the races; it's also to get under the skin of the sport and expose any malpractice. Because F1 is so technical and the aim is to push the boundaries, safeguarding intelligence is incredibly important and thus creates an obvious divide between the media and teams.

I wish I could have interviewed Eddie over the years as he's seen and done so much. Even now, every time I meet a driver it seems that Eddie has once employed him, which usually leads to a few gags about EJ being tight with his wages or still owing the driver a few quid. Few people realise that it was actually Eddie who gave Michael Schumacher his debut back in 1991, and other famous names he's employed include Rubens Barrichello, Jarno Trulli and 1996 world champion Damon Hill. I think this is the reason EJ gets away with so much and since he's worked with us his high-profile 'victims' have included Michael Schumacher, who he grabbed and dragged out of the garage; the Ferrari team boss Stefano Domenicali, who he lured in front of our cameras even though he was still on the phone; and there was the celebrated occasion he tried to go after Sebastian Vettel, only to be promptly thrown in the Red Bull pool in Monaco.

Though more reserved than Eddie, David has been great because the drivers feel safe when he is around – he has been one of them. When we first started working together, I'd ask David a question and he would pause for several seconds while he formulated the answer in his head. He would then start with the phrase, 'Well indeed, Jake', which was just his way of buying thinking time. I had to explain to him that this was no longer a case of a journalist asking a question to try and catch him out or put him in an awkward position, we were now a team and I wouldn't compromise him if he gave us his honest, genuine reactions. It was an interesting lesson for me, and a reminder that no matter how much pressure the drivers are under to be accessible and open with the media, the divide will always exist. Few drivers will ever actually enjoy doing the media side, even though they know it's important. David's approach was clever – he always said that in his mind he was paid to do the media stuff; the driving was what he did for free.

I love the fact that Eddie takes pleasure in being provocative and causing controversy. He rubs some people up the wrong way and generates endless debate among the sport's fans about his views. There is nothing worse than a pundit who is paid to have an opinion but doesn't give one – you certainly couldn't lay that charge at Eddie's door. He also has a keen sense of fun and decorum rarely comes into it. Take 2009 as a prime example. We're in the Brawn garage having just interviewed Jenson Button, and his mechanics are having a well-earned party. We were still live on the F1 Forum, so we went over to speak to them. They had linked arms, were having a beer and jumping around singing 'We Are The Champions'. Suddenly I looked across to see Eddie had joined in and was leading the celebrations, with complete disregard for the fact we were live to the nation. At exactly the same time you can see DC standing very straight, looking altogether more nervous and a little uncomfortable; perhaps the thought of EJ going even more wild was too much to take.

When I speak to Eddie about his first few years in the sport, I do wonder whether, as it's become more commercial and professional, it's lost some of the fun. There were days when drivers and media would all rub along together and there would be parties before, during and after the races. These days with Twitter, camera phones and social media, there seems to be more paranoia than ever before, and the distance between the media and the drivers has probably grown, even if the access remains excellent. Part of this is driven by corporate responsibility. Think back to the wild days of James Hunt, or the drivers' parties that were legendary in the 1960s – do you believe that the big businesses now associated with F1 would have tolerated that kind of madness? Nowadays, a race weekend won't pass by without the drivers having to go to a VIP area for a question-and-answer session, or to shake hands with dignitaries being shown around the garage. Whereas there are twenty or thirty footballers representing each club, only two drivers represent each team, and that, along with the large wages they earn, brings with it a certain duty. I don't feel sorry for the drivers that they have to adhere to pretty strict rules and not bring the team or the sponsors into disrepute. They are paid huge sums to be treated like kings and revered like gods, so to my mind it's totally acceptable that they should respect their paymasters.

As for the parties today, well there is still the odd crazy moment. After the 2012 Monaco Grand Prix Eddie rang me up and said, 'Head to Eze, bit of music, bit of madness.' When Eddie says 'bit of madness' you are usually better off giving it a wide berth, but I went along and his band were rocking out. So, the day after the Monaco GP I find myself singing along to EJ And The Robbers, as they're called, while Michael Fassbender takes time away from Hollywood to have a dance, and Roman Abramovich gets on his feet, clapping and dancing.

Only in EJ's world.

However, due to the demands of the sport, moments like that are few and far between. Perhaps in years gone by there was time to actually stop and smell the roses, but the calendar is now so packed that there simply isn't room in the schedule. As soon as the race is over the teams are dismantling the garages and packing away their motorhomes, usually because the next stop is thousands of miles away in just a few days' time.

One of the reasons that F1 is more of a commitment now than it was five, ten or twenty years ago is the way that the sport's footprint has quite clearly moved east. In 1992, the year Nigel Mansell was crowned world champion, there were sixteen races, of which ten were in Europe, none in the Middle East, and only one was in the Far East, in Japan. In 2012, we'll travel to twenty different races, eight of which are in Europe, two are in the Middle East and a whopping five are in the Far East: China, Malaysia, Singapore, Japan and Korea. Of course, this puts additional strain on the teams, the sponsors and media, who have to deal with greatly increased air miles and some pretty awful jetlag, but there is also a different ambience at many of the races.

Way back in 2004 it was reported that Bernie Ecclestone believed Europe would become a third-world continent eventually, and here we are, eight years later, trapped in a recession while in China sales of luxury cars are up around 40 per cent.

That's some foresight from Bernie. I understand that the facilities offered in places like Abu Dhabi are second to none, and that no one can put on a show as well run and professionally slick as Singapore, but for me many of these places still lack one thing. Atmosphere.

The problem with Formula One, I think, is that without an education in the sport and a real understanding of what is happening, it can seem dull. Even in modern F1, with all kinds of aids to help overtaking, it is still not uncommon, if a little rarer than it used to be, to see a processional race where it looks to the untrained eye like twenty-four cars driving around in a line with little or no excitement. Thankfully, though, the sport is aware that overtaking, unpredictability and excitement are what boost the viewing figures and, in turn, the value of F1. For example, at the start of the 2012 season the record of five different winners in the first five races was broken when Mark Webber won in Monaco, taking the new record to six different winners in six races. However, it's also worth bearing in mind that despite setting a new record for the unexpected, five of those first six races were won from the front of the grid. So it remains a fact that without huge amounts of overtaking or dramatic incidents, an audience unfamiliar with the nuances of the sport will struggle to recognise the subtle strategy decisions, the skills needed to preserve tyres or the brilliance it takes to keep a car at bay with defensive driving. I think in Europe and America most people have grown up being interested in some kind of motorsport, whether it's F1, NASCAR or MotoGP. But this isn't the case in the Middle East and in some parts of Asia. Therefore, in places such as China and Malaysia there is still a PR job to do to really get the people behind the sport and to fill the grandstands.

I honestly think that for Formula One to be seen by the global TV audience as the pinnacle of world motorsport, every seat in the grandstand needs to be full, the nearby cities need to be alive to the buzz of the F1 circus being in town, with the roar of the cars matched by the roar of the crowd. Sadly, in places such as South Korea and China, despite huge investment by these countries, we haven't witnessed such fervent support. I've wandered around Istanbul and Shanghai, and if I weren't there for work I truly wouldn't have known an F1 race was happening. I do wonder if it's good for the sport to branch out to pastures new as often as it has in recent seasons. Every year that I've presented F1 we've been to a new circuit, and with New York and Russia reportedly waiting in the wings, that doesn't look set to change any time soon.

There are clearly benefits for everyone involved in the sport. Take a look at the sponsors currently affiliated to F1 and you will see that a large number now come from the Middle East. It is where the money is, and in a sport that spends so much money, it's a valuable relationship to have.

I saw a report in 2010 which estimated the AVE – the Advertising Value Equivalent – for Red Bull after just six races of that season was a whopping $152 million. In other words, if Red Bull had to pay for similar exposure through advertising, they would have had to pay that figure. Other AVEs were reported as $46 million for Vodafone, who sponsored McLaren, and $35 million for Santander, who sponsored Ferrari. The teams also apply these measures to most of their media activity, such as driver announcements of sponsor appearances. The way they work out the value is to monitor the on-air exposure that each team generates, but only during a race. This is then calculated to work out the value. The 2010 report estimated that the average value for the fifteen major F1 sponsors at the time, involved from the front to the back of the grid, was $4 million per race for each and every one.

It is quite clear that if the Middle East is where the money is, then that is where the potential investors are, and therefore Formula One will naturally gravitate there. I just hope that the sport realises how important its past is too. Yes, the circuits in Europe don't look as glamorous, the paint might be peeling and the asphalt cracking, but nothing will ever take away the history that the likes of Monza, Silverstone and Spa can boast. Not to mention the fact that the traditional circuits still deliver dramatic and compelling racing.

Having said that, I loved travelling to India for its inaugural race; it seems to me to be one of the few countries that still feels individual and unique as the world becomes smaller and we all chase a standardised, safer-feeling planet. It has been a real privilege of this job to be able to see the world, but a small part of me dies every time I walk into a terminal building to be confronted by the same coffee chains and fast-food restau-rants in the arrivals hall. There were global brands in Delhi airport, of course, but as soon as we left the terminal it was clear that we were in a completely different culture. The sensory overload of noise and colour just added to the sense of occasion and my overriding memory was of travelling into the centre of Delhi to do some filming. Our priority for races such as India, which is a global first, is to try and take the people from their living rooms and transport them to where we are. Therefore we shot some film in the middle of town as they were preparing for Diwali, and EJ stuck to his entrepre-neurial roots by bartering for a new shirt, despite it being ludicrously cheap to start with.

Once we'd finished filming, I headed back to the circuit. I found myself sitting in a traffic jam – nothing uncommon in that, especially in a city like Delhi. But what was unusual was the fact that queuing alongside me in the traffic was a man on an elephant. I'll never forget it! One of the McLaren engineers managed to get a photo of two helmet-less men sharing a motorbike, both were looking at their phones, and their third passenger was a monkey the same size as them – now, you don't find that on the A43 as you approach Silverstone.

However, one of the difficulties was the poverty that we witnessed. I know that many of the locations we visit during the course of a season have various socio-economic and human rights issues, and I am generally a firm believer that you need to visit such places to give them the opportunity to change. But the poverty we saw in India was really hard to take, particularly as we were driving towards a multi-billion-rupee race track, with the world's most expensive and advanced racing cars entertaining the crowds. While it isn't Formula One's job to help countries solve these problems, perhaps something can be achieved by shining a light on concerns that exist.

Racing in Bahrain in 2012 was a troubling experience for many of us. I remember driving back to the hotel with barbed wire flanking the motorway, and one day on the way to the circuit I counted over forty police vehicles, not to mention the armoured cars and plenty of soldiers. It was the year following the Arab Spring and, having cancelled the race in 2011 because of unrest, there was intense scrutiny surrounding the decision to race there a year later. It was risky for the sport to take the chance, as all it needed was a protestor on the track or an attack on one of the drivers and there would have been some serious questions to answer.

In the event, the race passed off without too much incident. The Force India team did have a run-in with some protestors that led them to leave the track early on the Friday and miss one of the practice sessions. The following day in qualifying, despite an impressive performance, quite a few eyebrows were raised when the team hardly featured on the television coverage – most odd as the current Formula One TV coverage is the most professional it has ever been.

My clearest memory was of securing a rare broadcast

interview with Jean Todt, president of the FIA. I know we were covering a sports event, but at times like these I think people also look to the BBC to provide strong journalism. Myself, the cameraman and producer all entered Jean's very presidential-looking office at the circuit, complete with FIA flags and a large, imposing desk. As he sat down to begin the interview and I introduced myself to him, his press officer leaned in, looking a little concerned, and showed Jean something on his mobile phone. Jean stared at the phone, then picked up his own and looked as if he was dialling someone. He just sat there nodding his head, and I'm still not sure if he was making a call, or if he was simply buying himself some thinking time. But it soon became clear what he had been shown. The night before an alleged protestor was believed to have been shot dead by local security forces. This was bad news for a sport hoping that their presence in Bahrain wasn't going to garner negative headlines. It felt to me like a heck of a headline. Jean Todt is a well-practised interviewee, however, and managed to answer my questions with the confidence and assuredness of the most experienced politician. He stood by the FIA's verdict that it was indeed the right decision to race in Bahrain. It seemed to me important, though, to be the person asking him the tough questions.

On reflection I believe that Formula One accomplished something special by racing in Bahrain in 2012. Having been on the ground myself, there was no question that it was a kingdom with some serious social unrest. The Bahraini

authorities were having pressure applied by various govern-
ments and human rights groups during the race weekend,
and along with the high-profile hunger striker Abdulhadi
Abdulla Hubail Alkhawaja and the spotlight on the race, it
was a country under the microscope. The end result of the
race going ahead was that, while other countries such as Syria
and Libya were enduring what some would say was far worse
unrest and unimaginable suffering, the focus that weekend
was very much on Bahrain, because of the presence of Formula
One. The rolling-news channels transmitted plenty of shots
of rioters and protestors and, having been there for myself, I
actually believe that, notwithstanding the serious problems,
the story that F1 was in town gave the Bahrain situation far
greater prominence than it would otherwise have had. So,
despite many saying it was wrong to race in Bahrain at a time
when they had more important issues to be dealing with, in
effect I think the sport actually helped tell the country's story,
and gave the protestors' struggles global publicity.

Sadly, it is almost impossible for sport and politics to
remain separate from each other all the time, and there will be
times when certain races are contentious. However, I really
hope that, as Formula One pushes on to new frontiers, the
sport realises the importance of education, to tell the tale of
how F1 came to be so special and to inspire and fascinate the
drivers, bosses and engineers of the future, while at the same
time remembering its roots.

I understand that F1 is dependent on huge sums of money,

and that it has to chase that money, but I'd hate in fifty years, when I've long left the sport, to see the likes of Monza and Spa rundown and unused because of an obsession with countries that are currently awash with wealth and keen to host an event as powerful and prestigious as Formula One. Spa, Monza, Silverstone – they might not be shiny and perfect, but they are part of the fabric and history of the sport and that too has a value.

The sport has shown itself to be brave in the past. Despite facing huge international pressure to not race in South Africa during apartheid, F1 continued up until 1985, much to the disgust of some. There were heavy international sanctions in place, designed to isolate the country and force it to abandon its racist policies. However, Formula One was one of the last sports to abandon South Africa. James Hunt, the 1976 world champion, was reported to have launched into a withering attack on the South African authorities and the evils of apartheid while in the BBC commentary box. Apparently, as this was rather politically provocative content, the producer thought it wise to pass him a note that read: 'TALK ABOUT THE RACE!' Many also believe that the fact that F1 was quick to return in the 1990s was crucial to helping South Africa gain acceptance once again by the sporting world. And let's not forget that Formula One visited the stunning city of Budapest in 1986 – a significant moment as it was the first race to take place behind the Iron Curtain. It was the first time, because of politics, war and revolutions, that international motor racing had returned to Hungary in fifty years, and a huge crowd of 200,000 turned up, having travelled from all over Eastern Europe – what a coup by Bernie Ecclestone and the sport as a whole.

Probably the biggest question mark over Formula One, particularly when the global economy is suffering so badly, remains the costs involved. The issue with the sport will always be that developments and updates come at a price. Of course, the authorities could decide to impose a budget on all teams of just £1 million. It would make it affordable, but would it really be Formula One? Part of the attraction and the mystique are the astronomical sums involved, and I don't think you can hamstring the teams with a restriction. By its very nature, the sport forces the teams to take every minor part of the car and to improve it and develop it until it's the best in the field, and that is why it's always so inordinately expensive.

Teams will often grumble about the expense yet they will struggle to agree on any kind of budget cap or restrictions on what they can spend, as they too consider F1 to be as much an engineering battle as it is a racing one. Achieving a level playing field is a difficult problem to solve because the teams will always want to spend every penny available to make their car go faster. It is understandable that there is some frustration when the big teams spend millions developing parts that other teams simply can't match, such as the KERS unit. KERS, which stores energy under braking, is something that a few teams have spent huge sums on, whereas others can't afford to run it at all. Is this fair? Would a standardised KERS unit not be a better decision for the good of the sport? The problem here is that if you restrict spending on something like KERS, the teams will just channel the money they've saved into something else. Perhaps it's just inevitable that in F1 you will always have the rich and the not-so-rich. It's no different in football, where four or five clubs dominate the rest.

Having said that, even Ferrari – who have opened up a whole new Far Eastern market in recent years, which has been very lucrative, and are big spenders in the sport – realise the dangers that lie ahead. In June 2012, the Ferrari president, Luca di Montezemolo, declared that the sport cannot ignore Europe's financial meltdown, and, in his words, 'Drastic intervention is required. There is no longer the moment for getting bogged down in sterile discussions or the meanderings of engineers.' By this I imagine he means that the sport needs to look at the bigger picture, and while an engineer may love the chance to spend hundreds of hours and millions of pounds on one small element of the car, is that really a healthy approach? They are tough and impactful words, particularly from a team who will often spend big to win. Moves have already been made to keep costs under control, with the introduction of the rule in 2009 that teams can now use only eight engines per season – by contrast, back in the early 2000s a team could use nearly that many in a race weekend.

From driver safety to improving the show, Formula One has learned a lot over the years. But perhaps now its biggest battle is to alter the fundamental mindset of a sport that has often enjoyed a blank-cheque approach.

6

———

100,000 miles, 20 stops, 1 season

It's not just the teams and drivers in Formula One who are looking to evolve, change and improve at all times. The sport is also chasing the constant goal to remain the number one motorsport series in the world, which is a big reason why it has so many races in so many countries. In 2012 F1 had twenty races for the first time. This compares to just seven in 1950, the sport's inaugural season. These days, a whopping 100,000 miles separates the circuits over the course of a season, with many F1 personnel on the road almost constantly from March, when the season starts, until the champion is crowned and everyone returns home in November.

However, the coming of November by no means signifies the chance for everyone to relax. There are usually a couple of weeks for the teams to clear down at the end of the season and take their Christmas break, but come early January the sport is awash with glitzy car launches before it's off to the first test and the whole thing starts all over again for the next season. After that short winter pit stop, once a new season begins, it's non-stop, and very few people get a real insight into what is happening just to keep the show on the road. You know how it is when a good friend you haven't seen for months calls out of the blue and says, 'Surprise, I'm just down the road and thought I'd pop in for a cup of tea'? Suddenly your house is transformed into a hive of activity as you wash up, hoover, throw clutter into cupboards, clear surfaces, spray air freshener and plump up cushions. By the time the bell rings, you open the door with a huge smile and a casual comment such as, 'Oh, we were just relaxing on the sofa. Come on in, we've just put the kettle on anyway.' Well, that is what Formula One seems like to me. TV viewers, important guests and members of the media don't really see what goes on; they arrive in the pit lane or the paddock and it's like the sport has been there forever.

I can honestly say I've never walked into a Formula One paddock or pit lane and thought, 'What a mess.' They vary from place to place, of course, but they have a common theme that links them all. Perfection. At the 'fly-away' races – the term given to Grands Prix that happen outside of Europe – the teams have their own space in the paddock provided for them by the circuit. Even so, by Thursday morning, when the paddock bustles with activity, with journalists chasing stories and photographers snapping away, they will each have made their home their own – it's essentially a more impressive and expensive version of when you or I check into a hotel and put our smellies in the bathroom or a picture by the bed. The teams put branded walls up, so that merely by the colour you can tell which team's sandwiches you're eating; their own bespoke cutlery sits on clean tables, with pictures of their drivers by the door to welcome you; they will have flowers in their team colours adorning most surfaces; a menu printed up with various delicious food options, mood lighting, and sometimes some music is being played. None of them is short of food, drink or a warm welcome.

The garages by this stage are equally bespoke. On the television they look stunning: the drivers' names and graphics are on the floor, they have an engineers' area with multiple screens all feeding in essential data, TVs showing the action and computers for them to work on. There isn't an original garage wall in sight as they put up panelling so that the whole place is branded to look just like the garage they were in days before, at the previous Grand Prix. They use these team-coloured panels to build walls and rooms for their engineers or their drivers to meet in private comfort. Even at the back of the garage a security guard will man the entrance with a branded cordon to stop unwanted visitors and prying eyes.

On top of all this there are offices for team principals and drivers, media officers and engineers; each team has between fifty and eighty people, all helping to make each track just like the last. If you visited most venues outside the F1 weekend you'd find the building probably looked a little tired, cold and empty, and the garages would have exposed concrete walls and dusty grey floors, but Formula One is this great big multimillion-pound machine that moves around the world, stamping its unique and perfectly branded self on to often otherwise tired-looking circuits. The TV cameras are switched on and as the rich and famous arrive to see and be seen, it looks like the greatest place in the world to be. And often it is! But it takes some doing. Every single thing the teams use at the track is transported across the globe, from the race cars and the computers used to monitor unfolding races, to the office supplies and driver autograph cards. To add to the workload for the teams, the first four races of the year are in far-flung locations on the other side of the world.

The first stop of the season is traditionally Albert Park in the middle of Melbourne. It's autumn in the southern hemi-sphere, so not too hot, but the weather is generally great and as far as I'm concerned it's a fantastic time to be there. As for the race weekend itself, they certainly know how to do things! Albert Park is Melbourne's equivalent of Hyde Park in London or Central Park in New York. It's easy to get to, has stacks of great bars and restaurants all around, and to top it all off it's in the centre of a great city.

People often assume that my job is all glamour, but that's not the case at all – for example, I get to the first race of the year on a tram! It's quite strange arriving at a GP in the middle of a busy city. For Friday practice sessions the commute to work is shared with schoolchildren, shoppers, office workers and, of course, F1 fans, brimming with excitement and anticipation about the first race of the year. There is a real passion for racing in Australia, and it's also an incredibly important race for the teams. Melbourne isn't so much about the win and the points on offer; it's more to do with the fact that it is here that you'll find out whether your car is good, and if your season is likely to be a strong one. Only three times between 2000 and 2011 did the winner of the Australian Grand Prix not go on to be the world champion that year.

It's a fantastic way to start the season, partly because the Aussies pack the schedule with V8 supercars, celebrity races and all manner of other 'support races' on track, but also because attendances are often around 300,000 for the whole weekend. For the travelling circus of F1 it's also nice to be somewhere with a beach and a lively city. As you walk around in the evening or grab a quick few minutes' sunbathing time, you're guaranteed to bump into a few F1 personnel. That's what happens when F1 takes over a place!

However, no sooner have we all arrived in Melbourne than we head off to race two, which is on the outskirts of Kuala Lumpur, in Malaysia. These races are known in F1 circles as back-to-back races, and most people are on the plane first thing on Monday morning. Now this is a real test for car and driver. You may have had a car that can deal with the bumpy, confined track in a park in the middle of Melbourne, but will you also have the speed when that same car takes to the track in Malaysia? The Malaysian circuit, with its high-speed changes of direction and two of the longest straights in Formula One, is a complete contrast to Albert Park. And that's before you take into account the weather.

There is always the potential for some drama as far as the weather in Malaysia is concerned. In recent seasons, the race start time has been shifted so that the GP is on at a better time for European TV audiences. However, this also moves the race right into the middle of 'downpour time'. Every year we all gather at the entrance to the TV compound or in the paddock and marvel at how quickly the skies turn dark and menacing, and how sudden, hard and vicious the resulting downpour is. It is rain like you've never seen before, and it caused the 2009 and 2012 races to be stopped in their tracks.

Again, F1 comes prepared – as they say, 'Fail to prepare, prepare to fail.' And in this sport, an umbrella simply won't do. Nowadays, the teams pack instant gazebos with them, designed to be popped up over the cars on the grid in the event of a red-flag situation. F1 rules state that the cars must line up on the grid in the event of a red flag, so if it is raining and the stoppage lasts an hour, you end up with a very wet driver and car, not to mention a soaking for the millions of pounds of electrical hardware in and around a Formula One car.

What you do get with the Malaysian Grand Prix is plenty of contradictions. The urban modernity of Kuala Lumpur gives way to rural countryside as you approach the circuit;

there is blazing heat one moment, torrential rain the next; you can visit large, Western-style hotels yet across the road you can sit in a car park eating the local *nasi lemak*, cooked to order and costing just pennies.

At this point, after two races, a pattern has usually begun to emerge. The teams will have gathered thousands of separate pieces of information about their cars – which sections they're strong in, where they might be struggling. The drivers will have given all the feedback possible, the teams will have scraped and fought for every point on offer and now, after Malaysia, it's back to base, where they get their first breather of the year – not much of one, though, as by now the competition is intense. The gap is usually a two-week one, in which the teams can assemble their drivers, engineers, designers and the cars in one place for the first time and work on upgrading the car for the next race.

On average, cars are modified and updated throughout the season every 20 minutes, so just because there is a hiatus after the second race, during which there is no F1 on TV, the work is far from over. When the racing starts again it's another long-haul back-to-back trip, usually to China and then on to the kingdom of Bahrain, which was the first race to take place in the Middle East, in 2004. By the time we get to Bahrain, most people in F1 have seen more of each other for the past few weeks than they have their own families. It's an accepted part of the job and you have to go into it fully aware that the lifestyle is not the one of glamour that it may seem.

157

The other really tough thing about this part of the racing year is the constant battle with jetlag. I find Australia and China really tough: wide awake at 3am and almost too tired to speak by 4pm. And of course it affects the drivers too, who will therefore often try to lessen the effects by getting to races early or staying in that part of the world in between events rather than heading back to the UK. I remember Anthony Davidson, who was a British Formula One driver between 2002 and 2008, explaining to me how careful drivers need to be with jetlag. In 2005 he was a reserve driver for BAR Honda and had arrived at the track in Malaysia late in the week, as he was unlikely to be needed. As he was struggling to adjust to the time zone the news came through from the team that the Japanese driver Takuma Sato had gone down with a fever. The track layout is demanding for a driver in Malaysia, but it's the humidity that is the real tester; drivers lose kilos of fluid during the race and need to be in peak condition. Suddenly, a sleepy Anthony Davidson is told he's in the car, and the next thing he knows he's fighting a 200mph racing car as well as jetlag! He qualified a respectable fifteenth, but the following day his engine gave in after just two laps. Perhaps he went back to bed? He tells me he certainly decided from that day that he'd never arrive late at a track again, even if he was only the reserve driver.

Despite some of the drawbacks of travelling to different countries and between different time zones from one week to the next in the early season, there is one element of this phase

I love, and it's the flights. Not just because for most of them I can turn my phone off for a whole day, but also because it provides a great insight into the F1 'bubble': you can learn a lot about the psyches of the various teams and drivers when you're all travelling on the same plane. You'll arrive at Heathrow in early March each year, and straightaway you'll see familiar faces, try to avoid those who you forgot to send a Christmas card to and make a beeline for those you most want to sit next to for the next twenty-four hours. It's a bit like the first day back at school after the summer holidays.

On that first flight, every team is full of hope and anticipation. Drivers turn up looking tanned and fit, mechanics and engineers appear in their brand-new, perfectly clean and pressed team kit, ready to do all they can for their uniform, while the team principals will often make their way to sit towards the front of the plane. I imagine they're chatting to each other, trying their best to glean as much information as possible about the opposition without giving anything away themselves. The great unknown at the start of the season is one of the most exciting times for F1 – there's always masses of speculation, but hardly any facts or figures to base those stories on.

Sebastian Vettel described the first race of the season as the time when you finally have to 'pull your pants down and show what you've got'. In other words, after months of pre-season designing and testing behind closed garage doors, the truth is at last revealed. By the time we leave those first four races, anyone who hasn't got the speed, the reliability or both, knows the return to racing in Europe is the time to really improve things.

The arrival into the European leg of Formula One's season is where the big first raft of updates really starts to take place, and teams can begin to claw back any deficit to their rivals thanks to hard work at the factory. It's not only the cars that the teams spend their time and money transporting across Europe, though; the logistical job of moving all the gear needed to run a Formula One team is mindboggling. Once we get into Europe, the teams no longer have buildings provided for them; they now use their own. And we're not talking about a truck with a fold-down side and an awning – I mean vast, impressive displays of wealth and power that blow you away as you enter the paddock.

McLaren's is almost a direct copy of their Bond-like HQ. It has a huge, dark front where the people relaxing inside can look out at you and the paddock, but you can't see in. Very unnerving. It's spread over three floors, with an atrium in the middle looking right up to the top. It is very cool, modern and businesslike, with most people eating the delicious food on offer, or chatting over a coffee or glass of water. If you want to get a taste of the F1 party life, however, then pop next door to Red Bull. Their hospitality unit seems even bigger – a huge bar confronts you as you walk in, and it's not only energy drinks on offer! If you fancy a boozy afternoon, you can most certainly have one there. If you want to head upstairs, there is a restaurant area, a second bar serving tapas-style food, and also a roof terrace out at the back where you can overlook the track or, if you're not a racing fan, then just recline in the sunshine. Throw into the mix DJ decks, a retro design and some seriously good-looking people, and you know where to be seen. Even at the other end of the paddock, where teams are fighting hard to stay afloat and desperately trying to make their budget stretch to the end of the season, they understand the importance of entertainment. After all, that is what Formula One is.

But these buildings aren't only supplying somewhere to entertain the media and sponsors. They also provide offices for the marketing team, the team principal and the drivers. David Coulthard told me that when the Red Bull hospitality unit was first introduced, the drivers were blown away by the facilities. Plasma screens, colour-changing lights in the showers, massage tables – it was like a drivers' day-spa! Mind you, you have to be careful you don't let these pesky places catch you out. When I first started working in F1, I quickly got used to never having to actually open a door – up and down the paddock, everyone seemed to have those automatic sliding doors, to give the perfect initial impression of technological advancement. All was fine, until I went to walk into a particularly packed room one lunchtime – I leapt up the steps and slammed straight into the glass doors. Cue an almighty bang and the whole building shaking. Sadly, I'd chosen just about the only doors that you needed to slide manually. Fortunately my pride took a greater battering than my nose.

The only downside to these huge paddock palaces is that they are another thing that needs to be transported across the world. To every race, each team sends around a whopping 24 tonnes of equipment, which consists of a spare car chassis (in case one of the race cars has a problem), a few spare engines and gearboxes (for the same reason), plus all the other parts that make up each car. Add to that 500 metres of data cable, 300 metres of power cable, around 100 computers, 100 radios, office gear, chairs, tables, spare clothing, drivers' race suits and anything else an F1 team might just need over a weekend. All in all, it comes to well over 100 crates of stuff, a logistical nightmare that takes careful planning and preparation. Most teams have an inventory extending to some eighty pages to ensure nothing is forgotten.

Of course, if you're a successful team you end up adding to the incredible amounts of freight that you're transporting, because you have trophies to get back to the factory too! In 2009 we arrived in Valencia and while Jenson Button had won six races, his experienced Brazilian teammate Barrichello had yet to pick up a win. However, that day around the tight confines of the much-maligned Valencia street circuit he took the win and performed his famous Rubinho dance on the podium in the traditional way. Later that evening, about to board the F1 charter flight into Luton airport, I'm standing on the asphalt at Valencia airport with sun-kissed cheeks and heavy eyelids, and there it was, right next to me – the winner's trophy being carried by his race engineer. It was a tiny, cramped plane, but you can understand why the team didn't want to check the trophy into the hold, and so it travelled back with us in the cabin. It, too, had to queue at passport control until 1.30am, I am pleased to report!

But the logistics do not only affect the twelve Formula One teams. Pirelli, the F1 tyre supplier, have a motorhome that takes ten hours to build and eight hours to dismantle. In it, they serve over 25,000 meals per season, and cook 1,200km of pasta for their guests. As well as that, they will bring around 1,800 tyres to each race, with fifteen trucks and fifty staff.

With such mindboggling statistics, you can imagine the level of activity that the paddock and garages are thrown into once the race ends. As the cars slow down at the end of a Grand Prix, that is when the army of team personnel spring into action. The flag drops and in the garage the men who have built the car and delivered stunningly fast pit stops swap their race suits for lighter overalls, usually some music will be switched on, and the job of dismantling begins. Everything is taken apart according to strict instructions; usually in the garage the partition walls come down, then the pit-stop gear will be carefully packed away in bespoke cargo crates, designed by each team specifically to fit their equipment. Then the car's overhead system, which consists of lights, air-supply units, data cables, tyre-heating units and the power for the fans and monitors, will be disman-tled. At this point the pit lane and paddock are heaving with forklift trucks, as huge lorries start to get into position, ready to be loaded up. There's no time to hang around. After the 2012 Australian Grand Prix I went for a run around the track, and a few short hours after the circuit had been alive with F1 cars, there were now around thirty huge lorries rumbling along in convoy ready to depart Albert Park, leaving it to be cleared up and returned to normal.

The lorries will be packed with around 150 wheel rims; the engines will have been removed from the cars. Some parts will at this point be sent back to the factory for testing if they've reached the end of their natural life, while everything else is carefully dismantled, ready to serve the same purpose at the next Grand Prix. Finally, the car is covered and loaded on to the lorry and by around 10pm the work is done. Meanwhile, just a few feet away a similar operation is going on in the team's motorhome. They've cleared the tables and chairs, disconnected the power cables and cleaned the kitchens, showers, bars and terraces. The clever thing about the hospitality units is that they are designed to be packed into themselves, a bit like a Transformer. They go from an articulated lorry to a building that can seat between fifty and 200 people, and back to a lorry again at the end of the weekend.

Eventually it's time to leave, and time is of the essence for the teams. During the European season, when there is racing on successive weekends, there is usually seventy-two hours to go from serving coffee at one track to doing the same thing a few thousand miles away. The lorries will set off with a well-rested driver at the wheel, and a resting passenger who will travel with them for the next day or so. Once they arrive at their next destination, the whole process starts over again, but in reverse. Twenty-four hours to build and clean everything, ready for the eyes of the world.

By the Thursday leading up to the next race weekend, there are young women drinking cocktails, business meetings taking place over lunch and sponsor presentations with 100 guests, with most of the people in the building blissfully unaware of the journey it has been on for the past three days. And this is a tale repeated as Formula One crisscrosses Europe over the summer, usually kicking off in Barcelona.

While Melbourne is an important first test of a car's basic speed, the famous circuit in Barcelona deals out pretty much everything you can throw at an F1 car, so if you are fast around there the chances are your car is good. It requires good aerody-namic efficiency, slow-corner traction and high-speed grip, and for these reasons it's the place to test in the pre-season – the teams will have spent hundreds of hours and thousands of kilometres driving the track. The drivers know it intimately, so mistakes are rare, which means it's a true test of a car's ability. Sadly, though, it's rare to get a mixed-up grid and an exciting race here. But that doesn't bother the Spanish fans, who are amazing, and they often have a full pit lane for the official signing day on a Thursday. It's the first race of the season close to home, is usually blessed with stunning weather, and the modern, well-equipped circuit is just a short drive away from incredible, breathtaking Barcelona. It's pretty much perfect

– just bring ear plugs. Not for the noise of the cars, but the volume of the cheers when Fernando Alonso drives past!

After that it's on to Monaco, where we actually broadcast from the harbour because the tiny pit lane is just too cramped. On the flip side, here you can get up early on race day to walk the track. As the sun is rising, you can walk the very course that in a few hours will be alive to the sound of F1. Here, however, a motorhome isn't enough for Red Bull and they bring what has been dubbed a 'floatahome'. It's a huge barge that is sailed hundreds of miles to be moored in the harbour and comes complete with its own pool, which is the place to celebrate if Red Bull win the race – and into which I was thrown, fully clothed, by Mark Webber while I was interviewing him in 2011. The following day, after the race, Sebastian Vettel's win was followed by the most incredible party as all the Red Bull employees gathered around the pool and both Eddie Jordan and David Coulthard got a soaking.

The part of the season that really excites me is when we head to the historic double-header of Spa and Monza. Spa-Francorchamps is quite simply a motor-racing Mecca. High up in the Ardennes forest, surrounded by pretty yet indistinctive villages and at the mercy of the weather at any moment, this is what racing is all about. Forget the corporate world, the pristine modern circuits and the inner-city point-and-squirt circuits. Spa is F1 at its very best. The way to fully appreciate this race is by camping. It's certainly a favourite for most F1 fans and a way of really interacting with fellow racegoers – there are communal BBQs, huge flagpoles adorned with a favourite team or driver's colours, painted faces and sides of tents daubed with 'Schumacher Fan Club' or 'JB Rules'.

One of my favourite memories of working with the great Martin Brundle was when the two of us drove together to the track in 2010. We took Martin's E-Type and bumbled through south-east London, and through the Channel Tunnel, and past the scarred landscape of the First World War battlefields. Apart from some dodgy music choices by Martin, and a slight issue with exhaust fumes getting into the cockpit, it was a classic way to arrive at a classic race, in a classic car.

I've actually run the length of Spa, but only the once as it's a huge 7km track that feels like it's more uphill than it is down. It is vast and stretches away into the trees, just as circuits did in the classic racing era of the sixties and seventies. The most famous corner at Spa – almost the most famous in the world – is Eau Rouge. You have to see it to believe it. As you drive into the media car park, it looks like there is a fairground rollercoaster ride the other side of the trees; get closer and you realise it's the steep, aggressive hill that is Eau Rouge.

Monza also has a lot going for it as a track, although it's completely different from Spa, or in fact any other circuit on the calendar, and that merely adds to the magic. It's the fastest circuit in the world and cars are regularly brushing up against each other at speeds of over 200mph, but what really makes this place special is the fans. Although we have wonderfully loyal and knowledgable followers of F1 in the UK, the same is also true in Italy . . . as has always been the case. From the moment we arrive, on the Thursday morning, it's hard to move for people. They crowd around every entrance and exit hoping to spot their favourite driver or a famous face, and of course they are all resplendent in red! The circuit definitely lends itself to this kind of feverish support, and it is old, compact and classically chaotic in a very Italian way. Monza is an integral part of F1, and the *tifosi* are an integral part of Monza. They are the fanatical supporters who fill the campsites around the track, cheer and rejoice every time a Ferrari passes by, and they are also famous for heckling or booing all rivals to the team in red. Harmless, classic, F1 pantomime.

DC tells a great story about the time he retired at Monza during one year's Italian Grand Prix, when the car was suddenly surrounded by fans who proceeded to rip and grab any loose part to take home as souvenirs. He had to sprint away as he feared for his overalls . . . and his pants! The wonderful thing about Monza is that the fans are allowed on to the start–finish straight at the end of the race, and the podium sits over the track. The noise and the atmosphere are simply like nowhere else and if I were designing a circuit today, a podium in such a prominent position would be the first thing I would draw up.

After visiting nine different circuits in four months, the season remains unrelenting for the teams. At this stage, with just a few races left and the title likely to be won and lost in the near future, it's time to find the energy for one last push as the long-haul races return. Generally, I don't have the same love for the modern tracks as I do for the classics – they fail to stir me in the same way – but, for me, Singapore is an exception. What I love is that the race is so connected to the city around it; it doesn't feel like a race that is near a big financial centre, it's a race *in* a big financial centre. From going over the famous old Anderson Bridge, right past the Singapore Flyer big wheel to racing under an actual grandstand, it's the perfect example of where Formula One sees its future. My favourite view of the whole Grand Prix is the helicopter shot of F1 cars flying around tight, sharp corners while commuters on the flyover are heading home after a hard day's work.

The strange thing about this race from the point of view of our presenting team is that the sport remains on European time. As it's a night race it makes no sense for the drivers to be up at 8am and then still racing at midnight. Instead we all shift our day and wake at 1pm, work until about 3am, then head out for dinner and to bed by about five o'clock in the morning. It's very strange being in the middle of your working day at 10pm, yet it helps to create a slightly wild atmosphere and I think the teams and drivers feed off it to produce an entertaining spectacle. I certainly love it. The odd working hours do lead to a slightly limited choice of restaurants, however, so we often head to an awesome 'hawker food' area called Newton Circus.

Some say that eating is the national pastime in Singapore, and Newton Circus is perfect for gaining an insight into a traditional Singaporean way of eating. Hawker centres sprang up in the fifties and sixties and tend to be a group of places to eat, with communal seating, where the food is almost always cooked to order and definitely always tasty. The restaurants have a letter hanging outside them, either A, B, C or D, which corresponds to the cleanliness of the stall. It's a great way to experience 'real' Singapore and makes a nice change from the otherwise very strict, clean and regimented modern city.

In complete contrast, the F1 community then usually all board the same flight to Japan, another circuit that races under the 'classic' banner – it was here that Senna and Prost had their famous clashes in the late eighties and early nineties. One of my favourite things to do is run the track and stop at turn one, where they dramatically collided right at the start of the race in 1990, or perhaps the chicane at the end of the lap where they hit each other just a year later. I could almost still hear Murray Walker's voice and see those classic, grainy TV clips as I stood on the spot where history was made. To think that those moments now happened over twenty years ago gives me a strong sense of my own mortality.

The Japanese fans are great too. Being there in 2011, in the aftermath of the tsunami and the nuclear disaster, was really moving, and it was clear how grateful the Japanese were that the FIA had decided the country was safe. The Fukushima choir gave an emotional rendition of the national anthem, and after Jenson Button won the race that year he told us that it was his greatest ever victory, which is quite something when you consider his amazing career highlights over the years. His reaction was provoked not only by the struggles Japan had recently experienced, but also by his love for the country since he met his Japanese girlfriend Jessica. Suzuka, where the race is held, is itself a remarkable place as it was built by Honda as a test bed for their cars, making it an ideal circuit for the drivers to try out their skills on.

Formula One continues to break new barriers and travel to new frontiers, which it did when South Korea hosted its first race in 2010. The only real downside to our visit there was the lack of quality hotels, which meant we had to stay in what is locally referred to as a 'love motel'. I ended up causing quite a stir that first year when I tweeted that our hotel was rentable by the hour; a British tabloid then reported that it was a brothel and I returned to the hotel after the race to have two local news crews keen to interview me about my comments. I politely explained that as far as I was aware it was only available for young couples to use if they were already an item but that, even so, it wasn't what we were used to in Europe. I'm no prude, but it was quite an education!

Abu Dhabi is another new circuit that both the teams and the fans have taken to. Unfortunately, its design doesn't lend itself to overtaking-filled races, but nevertheless I can vouch from personal experience that it's an exciting track when you're the one doing the driving. I once filmed a feature for the BBC in which I had to follow the ex-F1 racer Jean Alesi around the track in a single seater that was probably a tenth as powerful and aggressive as an F1 car. I was doing okay, keeping up as he went around relatively slowly so that we got used to the track. Then he went for it – albeit at a friendly speed and in a car much slower than F1, and in single file and not racing. On the main straight it felt like my helmet was being sucked from my head, around the corners I was barely able to see as the car shook me from side to side, and after trying to keep up and not being used to the speed I was carrying, I made a bad entry to one corner which then put me out of position in the next and I was lucky not to end up in the barriers. A good reminder as to why they do the driving and I do the talking!

Abu Dhabi is also a race I'd recommend if you fancy doing some celeb-spotting. We often get famous faces on the show, from Hugh Grant to Rowan Atkinson to George Lucas. My highlight, however, was Paul McCartney (my dad is a huge Beatles fan – my mum claims he still hasn't fully recovered from John Lennon's death), with whom we managed to get an interview at the Yas Island circuit at the end of the 2011 season. Had I been walking down the street and bumped into Sir Paul, I would have been dumbfounded and unable to speak; however, when I'm on live TV with so many things to think about, I rarely get star-struck or have an awareness of what is actually happening. But I'll never forget finishing the interview with Paul, thanking him as he left us and moving on to introduce a VT. Eddie Jordan and I just looked at each other with wild eyes and expressions that said, 'I don't believe it!' I was completely awestruck, buzzing from the thrill of having just interviewed a Beatle, when EJ came out with the immortal line: 'Did I call him George?' Sadly Eddie had. It went viral and became an internet sensation, and people chanted 'George' at EJ for the rest of the weekend.

Having spent nine months traversing continents, visiting both the classic, atmospheric circuits and the modern, pristine tracks, it's only right that we finish the year at one of the most emotional and evocative venues of them all, Interlagos, in Sao Paulo, for the Brazilian Grand Prix. The paint is peeling off, the track has cracks in it, the entrance looks just as it did in the 1980s and there are mementos of the past everywhere . . . and that is why the F1 world loves going racing there. It's a truly stunning venue in a wild city. People who have been to Rio will tell you that Sao Paulo isn't as beautiful, as cultured or as exciting, but I can tell you that it is well worth the trip nevertheless. Reminders of Ayrton Senna are all-pervasive, from street names to buildings, to pictures at the track. F1 has never seen, and probably never will, another driver like Senna. He captivated the world, he drove on the limit, he put honest emotion ahead of sponsors' commitments, and he was a true champion. The success of the *Senna* movie is a testament to how much the world revelled in his success, and how much respect it has for the way he achieved it.

Because so little has changed at Interlagos since Senna's day, you can still conjure images of the grandstands roaring his name, and still stand in the very places that he did when he felt some of his most raw and powerful emotions. I remember standing on the start–finish straight in 2011, imagining just how much he would have given to see the track today – he wouldn't believe the love that Brazil still has for him. I often feel for his nephew Bruno, who has such a weight of expectation on his shoulders and who will always struggle to live up to the Senna name. How can you? However, he remains one of the most approachable, friendly and accessible drivers in the sport, and that says a lot about how grounded he is.

In 2009 I visited the favelas with Lewis Hamilton. Standing high on the hills above the city, overlooking the shanty towns where millions of people live, you can see the track and hear the cars. Can you imagine how much inspiration the local children would have taken from hearing the car of their hero Ayrton reverberating around the ramshackle buildings? There is such passion for F1 in Brazil, and you really feel part of something special when you are there. The race signifies the end of a gruelling season for drivers, teams and the media, who have all played their part in this huge, well-oiled travelling circus that has delivered drama and entertainment across various countries and continents since the start of the season.

Being F1, there is always room for a party and the last flight of the year is often a chance for everyone to unwind and breathe a sigh of relief after all the hard work. I remember the end of the 2009 season, when Jenson Button had just clinched the world title in Brazil but it was Mark Webber who had won the actual race. Jenson may have grabbed the headlines, but it was a stunning drive for Mark and he certainly helped that transatlantic flight fly by with his celebrations. He was jubilant not only because the win set him up for the following season but also because Interlagos is one of the 'big ones' in the eyes of the drivers. Silverstone, Monaco, Monza, Spa and Interlagos are the 'classics' and victory at one of these tracks means that little bit more than the rest. On that flight home, Mark's delight showed how much it meant to him.

7

Britain, Britain, Britain

I find it remarkable that so few people realise just how influential Britain has been for motor racing in general and Formula One in particular. And I'm not just talking about the sport in the modern era; I mean the very existence of it. In fact, Formula One was born at a certain former airfield in Northamptonshire that you might just have heard of, called Silverstone. These days, when a new circuit joins the Formula One calendar, the track design is a multimillion-pound job in which the engineers look at ways to build a circuit that produces racing that is both exciting and safe, and they often take their inspiration from some of the best parts of the best circuits around the world before embarking on development projects that last many months.

It sometimes feels as though each new circuit strives to outdo the last. Singapore had the first night-time race, China the biggest grandstand, South Korea the longest straight. In 2012 the Circuit of the Americas joined the fun; at a huge cost, ten feet of clay was excavated out of the dry Texas desert and thousands of cubic feet of material was laid in its place along the full length of the three-and-a-half-mile track in order to build a state-of-the-art F1 race circuit. Suffice it to say, things were a little different in the 1940s.

Back in the mid-forties Silverstone was well used to the rippling rasp of a powerful engine, only not those belonging to Formula One cars. At this time the place we now call 'The Home of British Motor Racing' was the base of RAF Silverstone, and during the Second World War it was where No. 17 Operational Training Unit, who flew the Vickers Wellington bomber, were stationed. It was a large airfield, in the typical Class A layout with three separate runways. Even today, when we're busy working in the TV compound and transmitting a modern F1 race across the world, all we need to do is look out of the office window to be reminded of the history of the place: the giant writing and paint marks on the ground, which would have once guided the pilots to the right runway, are still visible.

So how did the airfield go from heavyweight bombers to lightweight racing cars? The story goes that in 1947 a local man called Maurice Geoghegan, who lived in the village of Silverstone, noticed that the post-war airfield was just deserted asphalt. To any petrol-head, that is simply an invitation to go racing! Maurice and eleven other drivers apparently headed down to the track one afternoon and created their own two-mile circuit. Little did they know then that they had started something that would be going strong well over sixty years later, with hundreds of thousands of spectators and the eyes of the world trained on it every year.

On that day it seemed that Maurice himself had other things on his mind, however, as he allegedly wrote off his car by running over a sheep and killing the poor animal. A good example of just how much things have changed! This inaugural race went down in history as the Mutton Grand Prix. The following year the Royal Automobile Club (RAC) took on a lease for the circuit and started to formalise things, setting up a proper racing circuit and making use of the runways themselves. Even at this stage, as they raced along the runways and then out on to the perimeter circuit, they were already using names we all recognise today – Hangar Straight, Club, Woodcote and Copse all featured.

But it was from 1949 and onwards that the track started to take the shape that is more or less still used today. That year they held an International Trophy race and the likes of Alberto Ascari and Giuseppe Farina came to Britain to pit their wits against each other and entertain the crowds, and decided to race using the perimeter road around the circuit. Even then, the dangers of racing were apparent with the death of St John Horsfall in the final race.

Finally, in 1950, Formula One was born, and Silverstone was chosen as the very first place to hold a race, kick-starting that inaugural F1 championship season. It was described at the time as 'a great and colourful day for British motorsport' and attracted around 100,000 spectators. Not only that, the king and queen were also in attendance, the first time the reigning sovereign had attended a motor race in Great Britain. The excitement must have been intense among the crowd and the royal guests that day as Alfa Romeo and Maserati racing cars, piloted by famous international drivers, lined up on the grid. All that separated the public from the track in those days were a few straw bales and a rope line.

That first race was an emphatic demonstration of the power and poise that Alfa Romeo cars boasted in that era. They were so dominant on that sunny, warm, English afternoon that the only three cars to finish the race on the lead lap were all Alfa Romeos. Local hero Reg Parnell finished third behind the Italian pairing of Luigi Fagioli and the race winner, the great Giuseppe Farina, who ended the year as the first ever Formula One world champion. Even in those days the Alfas flashed past the crowd, the royal party and the old RAF buildings at well over 100mph, a true display of post-war engineering and elegance. In his victory speech, Farina announced to the crowd, 'I have one great desire, to come to Silverstone again and again' – and so he did, as have crowds, cars and drivers for decades since.

Since those bygone days, when all a driver had to keep

179

himself safe was a hay bale and a large slice of luck, the sport has, of course, changed beyond all recognition, yet Britain has remained central to the story. Despite the Middle East and the Far East becoming ever more familiar parts of the Formula One circus, and the economic boom of China and the car-building, technologically advanced Japan, Britain has remained integral to Formula One – to this day, the majority of cars making up the F1 field are British built and British designed.

While F1 owes a great debt of gratitude to the skill and brilliance of engineers, mechanics and business brains born on this small island, it has not been a one-way street: the sport has also done a great deal for the British economy. The success of the brilliant minds of people such as Adrian Newey and Ross Brawn, who are building cars and winning current F1 races, inspires the next generation of engineers who will take on the role of pushing the envelope in the sport's never-ending quest for speed. The future seems guaranteed and, in fact, there are currently more than fifteen British universities offering motorsport engineering and management degrees, testament to the rewards that can be reaped by a life and career in a motorsport.

It is estimated that Formula One and motorsport is worth a corking £6 billion to the UK economy. Britain retains its mantle as the 'Home of Formula One' in part due to the area in southern England known within the sport as 'Motorsport Valley'. The cluster of more than 4,500 companies employs over 25,000 highly qualified engineers and many of them work for F1 teams that you might not necessarily think were based in Britain. Many people look at the Renault team, which the flamboyant Italian Flavio Briatore ran, and think they must be the French team of F1. Do they build their car in Lyon or perhaps Marseille? *Non!* In fact, as they were celebrating winning World Championship trophies with Fernando Alonso in 2005 and 2006, the village of Enstone in Oxfordshire was where most of the rejoicing could be found. To this day they exist as the Lotus team, still drawing on skills from the surrounding area.

What of Mercedes? It was a big step for the German car giant to decide that they would enter Formula One back in 2010. In the preceding years the sport had lost big-budget car manufacturers such as Toyota, Honda and BMW, yet the decision was taken to recreate the 'Silver Arrows' team, fifty-five years after they last competed and won. They returned with two German drivers in the shape of Nico Rosberg, son of the 1982 world champion Keke, and seven-time champion Michael Schumacher. I went to their museum in Stuttgart for their great unveiling at the start of that 2010 season. Not far from Stuttgart's famous football stadium stands an eye-catching tribute to the remarkable success of Mercedes. It's even on Mercedes Street! All silver, steel and glass, it is a modern memorial to the great things they have achieved in the past, such as winning F1 championships with the great Juan Manuel Fangio, as well as to the road cars they build and design today. I interviewed Michael that morning, with news of his return to F1, billed as one of the most famous sporting comebacks ever, dominating all the bulletins. He had retired from F1 three years earlier and now, in his forties, he was set to try the seemingly impossible and return to one of the most physically and mentally demanding sports there is.

As I stood there asking him about the motivation for his comeback and he was wearing the all-silver race suit of Mercedes Benz, I recalled interviewing him in 2009 at the German Grand Prix in the company of David Coulthard and Eddie Jordan. The three of them had been reminiscing about Eddie giving Schumacher his first drive, and David and he were laughing about the time they had a big crash in Spa which resulted in Michael searching DC out in the pit lane with his fists at the ready because he'd thought DC had deliberately slowed in front of him and caused the accident. At the end of that interview in 2009 I had quizzed Michael about returning to the sport. He had been indulging his passion for speed with motorbikes, but had suffered an accident that had damaged his neck. I asked him whether he was having two-wheel fun because he was missing the thrill of F1 competition. He fixed me with that familiar icy stare and categorically denied he was keen on a return to F1. Eight months later, there I was interviewing him in front of the car he'd be driving in 2010. Funny old world. He and Nico both referred to Mercedes as the German national team that day; a German marque, two German drivers, being launched in Germany.

But where was their car designed, developed and built? In a nondescript factory just off the A43 on the outskirts of Brackley in Northamptonshire.

If you ever drive past, it's worth just pulling off the road to see where they are based, as the design offices and wind tunnels that these days are building cars in the name of Mercedes have a long association with the sport. It was home to the BAR F1 team before becoming Honda, then was afterwards renamed as Brawn and now finally Mercedes. Despite peaks and troughs of performance, race wins and championship trophies, none of the teams over the years decided to relocate the factory away from Motorsport Valley, or even outside of the UK – the greatest endorsement of the talent, and facilities, at their disposal.

In fact, it's a similar story at the HQ of the most successful team in recent years, Red Bull. The soft-drinks magnate Dietrich Mateschitz may own his own racing circuit in his native Austria; he might have enough money to base his F1 team anywhere in the world, but Milton Keynes is his team's chosen home. Even their base has a stellar F1 past. It was home to Stewart Grand Prix in 1997, then it was reborn three years later as Jaguar, before finally being bought by Red Bull.

Strikingly, despite Formula One being the ultimate global sport, between 2005 and 2011 the championship-winning driver had his car built in Britain every season bar one. And, of the twelve teams that are currently competing, only HRT, Sauber, Toro Rosso and Ferrari are not 'made in Britain'. All these things make, in my opinion, the British Grand Prix at Silverstone the most important race of them all. Home is nearby to most of the teams, and the hundreds of thousands or more who turn up each year are walking in the historic footsteps of those very first motorsport lovers over sixty years before.

Alain Prost was the master of Silverstone in the 1980s, winning the race five times between 1983 and 1993 (his record is matched only by Jim Clark, who also notched five British Grand Prix wins, though not all of his were at Silverstone, of course, as in his day Aintree and Brands Hatch also hosted the race), but the first British driver to win the British Grand Prix at Silverstone was Peter Collins. Compared to other men who have pulled on a racing helmet and taken to the track in the name of British racing, he wouldn't be regarded as one of the most celebrated. Yet in his short career of just thirty-five races in Formula One, he managed three wins and nine podiums, and will forever be remembered as the first British driver to stand on the top step of the Silverstone podium in 1958. Sadly, later that year the curse of F1 struck again when Peter crashed at the Nurburgring in Germany and died shortly afterwards from his injuries.

Nigel Mansell's legendary race at Silverstone in 1992 has gone down in F1 folklore, though more for what happened after the chequered flag went down than for what happened during the race. As Mansell made his way around the final couple of corners, Murray Walker announced, 'They love him and he loves them', in reference to the fans who had become besotted with 'Our Nige' around that time. As Nigel crosses the finish line you can just make out tiny figures appearing from all over the circuit, ducking under fences, climbing over barriers . . . all of them surging towards Nigel.

Who knows if it was a planned celebration or merely an example of the affection the fans felt for Nigel, but clearly Murray didn't approve of their actions. In reality it was pretty dangerous. Nigel had finished the race as winner, but behind him the likes of Gerhard Berger, Michael Schumacher and Martin Brundle were still fighting for places, so thank goodness the fans mainly kept off the track. Eventually one of them managed to get a flag into Mansell's hand, and the shot of them all leaping for joy around his car and Nigel in his blue and yellow Williams driving around at a crawl, flag in hand, is now an iconic one. That year he went on to become the Formula One world champion, and who knows how much of the inspiration for that came from the passion of the crowd on that sunny Silverstone afternoon.

More recently it was another British driver who announced himself to the British racing fans with an incredible drive at Silverstone. Over the years, Silverstone has developed something of a reputation for being wind lashed and rain soaked, and while you can never rely on the British summer it's an unfair stereotype in many respects. Having said that, back in 2008 it was most certainly wet, and one man rose above his opposition, and the weather, to tame the track and take his first home win. That man was Lewis Hamilton.

In 2008 Lewis arrived at Silverstone under a fair amount of pressure. It may have been only his second Formula One season, but such was his impact on the sport that he was already being spoken about as a future world champion. In fact, he'd spent much of his second season as the championship leader after picking up famous wins in Australia and then Monaco. However, in recent races, Lewis had fallen from first to fourth in the drivers' standings and had failed to score points in the previous two races. Not only that, he'd crashed into the back of Kimi Raikkonen in the pit lane in Canada, then taken a grid-place penalty and suffered a penalty for overtaking Sebastian Vettel by missing a chicane in the preceding races. Lewis had already been feeling the heat, and suddenly here he was on home soil with all eyes trained on him as the great hope for a British win that weekend.

However, in Saturday's qualifying session Lewis had slid into the gravel, before seemingly taking a more conservative approach to the second flying lap which left him fourth on the grid, with his teammate, Heikki Kovalainen, finding the speed to take pole. Come race day Lewis had it all to do. Sunday afternoon, 1pm, and the lights go out for the start of the race. On a wet, slippery track Lewis gets a breathtaking start and takes the lead, but then his teammate fights back to retake the advantage. It was tough going in the conditions. Mark Webber spun in the rain; Felipe Massa lost control of his car, too, on the wet track; while David Coulthard and Sebastian Vettel hit each other and both retired.

Eventually on lap five Lewis made the pass on his team-mate, and there began the most incredible drive. By lap ten Lewis had managed to create a 6-second gap between himself and the car behind. By lap thirty-eight, as others toiled, he had built his lead up to 36 seconds. By the time the race was nearing the end, his title rival Felipe Massa had spun an incredible five times, and only thirteen cars of the twenty finished the race, an illustration of how tough the conditions were. Hamilton emerged through a wall of spray and rain to win the race by an astonishing 68 seconds, the largest margin of victory in a Formula One race since 1995. It put Lewis back at the top of the drivers' standings, and just like Nigel, he too went on to become that year's drivers' champion. Who knows, perhaps Silverstone is something of a lucky charm . . .

I've seen the circuit from a fair few angles, too. I've floated over it in the early morning in a hot-air balloon with Eddie Jordan, who decided he was hungry after we landed and started flagging down passing cars for directions; such is the regular appearance of F1 folk in this part of the world, though, that no one even gave him a second look as they directed us to a nearby pub for a full English breakfast. And I've circled the track in Martin Brundle's helicopter, as he regaled me with tales of his early years watching from the banking and falling in love with the sport that he'd one day be so involved with. But my favourite trip around the circuit was on a humble bike, and for me that day summed up all that is great about the British Grand Prix.

It was the Thursday morning of the 2011 Formula One race, and the British weather was living up to its image. It was grey, cold, the morning mist was just beginning to lift, and I was trying to co-ordinate myself, David and Eddie on the same bike. It was a two-wheeled, three-man affair and I was responsible for steering and braking – not the easiest of tasks!

As we stood by the bike taking directions from the production team, to our left there was a steady stream of traffic, forming a snake of cars and caravans as far as the eye could see. A small country lane by the village of Silverstone, which would usually be interrupted at nine o'clock on a Thursday morning only by the sound of birds singing or tractors rumbling by, was alive to the buzz of British Grand Prix week. Cars full of young lads with little tents and a lot of beer passed us by; elderly couples who had probably been coming to watch the racing since before they were married; families with kids in the back gearing up for their first taste of a Formula One car at full speed. Hen parties, stag dos, work trips, once-in-a-lifetime treats – everyone was full of excitement as their wide eyes took in the surroundings, and almost to a car they tooted their horn and gave us a wave.

Before long we were cycling through campsites and people emerged to see what the fuss was about. We chatted to a couple who had been to the race every year since the 1960s, met numerous teenagers who said they'd been as babies and had never missed a race since, and almost everyone had a story to tell about their own personal British Grand Prix high-light. No surprise, really, when there have been so many.

The weather was certainly being kind to us that day. The mist cleared and there was not a cloud in the sky as we left the campsites. We meandered through a few villages and knocked on the door of the house where Eddie Jordan once lived. He told us that such was his desire to race and his belief that he could make it a success that his wife Marie worked at the local vegetable-packing factory to help pay the bills so he could indulge his passion. It seemed every street around us had a connection to the sport. Either a team member was living there or used to live there, or someone's child was at school with another whose dad works in F1.

In all honesty, only at this moment did I realise how much Formula One means to people in the UK. They might not have the time or money to visit twenty, ten or even one race a year, but through their televisions they tune in to a sport that seems to resonate with that whole area, indeed with the whole country.

Eventually we made it to the circuit. Despite its status as the oldest F1 circuit of them all, Silverstone, like anywhere, has had to move with the times. Silverstone hasn't been without its problems over the years and some were critical of the lack of development or investment in the track – not helped by events such as the Easter weekend wash-out of 2000 when the car parks were turned into unusable quagmires by the deluge and queues stretched for miles with many ticket-holders unable to make it in to see the race, a scene sadly reported in 2012.

Four years later the then president of the British Racing Drivers' Club (BRDC), Sir Jackie Stewart, announced that the British Grand Prix would not be included on the 2005 provisional calendar and therefore a Silverstone race was unlikely. In the December of that year it was decided the race would go ahead, much to the relief of British F1 fans, but in 2008 it emerged that a long-term deal to move the race to Donington Park had been agreed and that the 2009 British Grand Prix at Silverstone would, indeed, be the last there for the foreseeable future. I hosted the race that weekend and had so many conversations with people about what Silverstone means to British racing and how sad it was that its time was up.

However, details then started to emerge from Donington Park that all was not well. I recall plenty of interviews in which Donington's developers made it clear they were on schedule and had the funds to pull off the job, as the circuit needed considerable development if it were to host Formula One. Then, in late 2009, it was reported that Donington had failed to raise the £130 million they needed to stage the race. Gradually, the name Silverstone began to be mentioned again, until it came to pass that the circuit's owners, the BRDC, did a deal with Bernie Ecclestone to host the race for the next seventeen years. It was a huge commitment for both sides, but Silverstone were adamant that they needed a long-term deal if they were to carry out the required redevelopment of the circuit.

I was delighted when I saw the news. I think it's great that the likes of Abu Dhabi, India and Singapore are pushing the geographic boundaries of the sport, but you also need the context provided by the classic circuits such as Silverstone, Spa and Monza, which are often also those that provide the biggest test for the drivers and their cars.

It is important that the sport's owners prevent the calendar from going stale, and that they increase the sport's global profile, but there must always be a place for the circuits that provide a different thrill for competitors and fans. The older tracks, in Silverstone's case owned by private members, have to make the maths work. Some of the new circuits are government backed, of course, but the only real way to recoup the cost of hosting a race is with ticket sales. The seventeen-year Silverstone deal will cost the BRDC millions of pounds and they do not control trackside advertising or TV rights, so tickets are key and that's why the wonderful, loyal British spectators are so central to the story – without their support and participation, there is no British Grand Prix.

Fortunately, the fans' enthusiasm looks in no way about to falter and there is definitely still a true sense of motoring passion and pedigree among them. Come rain or shine they are positive and excited, and you really get an awareness of what it means to them to be at their home race. They'll happily sit on a picnic chair for hours with a flask and a sand-wich, just to see or hear an F1 car. It's great that camping is a big part of this particular race. I normally drive to the track at about 8am on a Sunday and I pass hundreds of campers walking up to 5 miles to get to the circuit. I've often stopped and asked if they'd like a lift, to which they usually reply, 'No thanks, walking is part of the day.' Magic.

Even in terrible weather, you can't put the fans off. Practice sessions can actually be notoriously dry, with cars just endlessly going round in circles, carrying out whatever work the team has asked the driver to perform. There is no overtaking, no dramatic race start and no one is pushing to deliver a stunning lap before the flag drops. There isn't a celebration and not a droplet of champagne is sprayed into the air, yet despite all that the fans turn up in their thousands. I remember in 2011 there was horrible weather for Friday practice, so Eddie and I decided to go and thank the loyal F1 lovers by heading out to one of the public concourses and selling a few ice creams. It was raining, but we figured that if anyone could sell ice creams in the rain Eddie could!

As we headed towards the ice-cream van and its very accommodating owner, it was amazing to see families huddled under umbrellas eating fish and chips, couples sitting on plastic bags looking at the photos they'd taken and groups of mates filling the grandstands. It was completely ludicrous, as it was cold and rain was driving down, but equally it was just brilliantly British and a great example of the passion we have for sport – a bit of wet stuff won't put us off! As for Eddie, he was in his element and clearly hasn't forgotten his days as a salesman. I guess whether it's persuading DHL to spend money sponsoring his F1 team, or convincing a drenched and shivering member of the public to part with £1.50 for an ice cream in the cold, it's a similar story. We sold cones to a family whose two kids were called Damon and Jordan. There was a teenager whose first name was Nigel, middle name Mansell. And also a woman, born in 1962, who was delivered on the way home from a race, her mum having gone into labour as they were driving home. She's now a huge F1 fan herself and was there with the masses, enjoying the day, if not the rain.

There's one incident above all others that has brought home to me the spirit of family and community that exists in Formula One and unites fans and teams alike. In Spain in 2012 we were live on air and heading towards the Williams garage to interview the race winner Pastor Maldonado. It was a memorable day for Williams, who had won their first Formula One race since the Brazilian Grand Prix in 2004. Not only that, the victory had come just five races into the season, helping to banish memories of the year before which had been nothing short of a disaster for Williams – it was their worst ever season in the sport, with just five points won and ninth their best finish. To cap it all, Pastor Maldonado scored just a solitary point, making him statistically the worst driver in the team's long and illustrious history.

Therefore the wild abandon in the Williams camp when they took pole on the Saturday in Barcelona was understandable, and especially as they followed up by leading much of the way to the chequered flag as Fernando Alonso tried, and failed, to keep tabs on the Venezuelan driver.

To make things even more special that weekend, one of the sport's most lovable characters, Sir Frank Williams himself, a man who lives and breathes motor racing, was celebrating his 70th birthday. On the Saturday night there had been a big party for him in the team motorhome, so it was great that the team were also toasting a remarkable, if unexpected, pole position. The race weekend was the 'perfect storm' in Formula One's eyes: a driver many didn't think was up to the job, a team people thought would be lucky ever to taste victory champagne again and a team owner who was now enjoying double celebrations.

One of the traditions after a race win is for the team to gather, drink a glass of fizz and pose for the obligatory photo that will forever be a reminder of a hard-fought victory. So, a couple of hours after the race, the team assembled in the Williams garage, and Frank gave a short speech to thank them for their hard work. Just moments after the team had stopped to reflect on the achievements of the day, however, their joy was replaced with panic. Somehow fuel had ignited at the back of the busy garage, and with so much technical equipment, extra fuel drums, carbon fibre, plastic and other electrical and flammable gear around, it quickly turned into a terrifying scene as thick, jet-black smoke billowed out of the garage, filling the Spanish pit lane and paddock with horrible, acrid fumes.

We were about 30 feet away and live on air when we saw the smoke rising above the paddock buildings; at first we thought it was some kind of celebration, or perhaps even a kitchen fire. The team garages these days are so well controlled and monitored that despite the dangers that obviously exist, they are actually very safe places to work due to the diligence and professionalism of the team personnel. It was a real shock, then, to realise this was a garage fire, the kind of thing most of the pit lane have never seen before. Therefore, it was brilliant to see how well people reacted, and what really struck a chord with me was that it was Williams's opponents – their rivals, their competitors – who sprang to their assistance.

Thankfully, Sir Frank Williams was very quickly evacuated from the garage, most people had managed to sprint to safety, and the injuries were mercifully minor on the whole. And that really was thanks to the F1 community, the men and women who've spent years working together, whether for the same team or moving from team to team up and down the pit lane. The image of mechanics holding huge, powerful water hoses will live with me forever, specifically because just one hose was held by men from no fewer than four different teams.

It's not only the expertise of our engineers, the skill of our drivers, the atmosphere of our race tracks, the unfaltering enthusiasm of our supporters and the sense of community that all these things foster that make Britain so integral to the sport of Formula One. The UK has also delivered us some of the most famous and celebrated commentators and experts ever to have watched the sport and helped to bring it alive for the millions at home who tune in every weekend.

It's staggering to think that nowadays we broadcast for around twelve hours live each weekend, but that up until the mid-1990s you were lucky if every race was live and in full. It seems that no matter how much the coverage increases, the capacity of the British fans to absorb it also knows no limits. Anyone who has ever stood with a microphone in the pit lane or settled into the chair behind the microphone in the commentary box has taken on a great responsibility. Formula One isn't just wallpaper TV; it's not broadcasting that people watch to fill a gap, it's appointment-to-view television and therefore with broadcasting it comes great responsibility. And yet the BBC decided to employ Eddie Jordan! I jest, of course, but the thrill for Eddie, David and me is that when you are talking about teams who have spent millions and drivers who have sacrificed so much to get to the top of their chosen field, it actually means something. Shows that give away a few quid are fun, comedies and dramas are important to the broadcasting landscape, and talent shows and reality TV clearly entertain the masses. But few programmes will bring you the drama second by second, building to the moment when someone is crowned a world champion. It's drama without a script, a talent show without a public vote. Broadcasting that kind of TV can be a nerve-wracking experience, but thankfully alongside me are two current stars of the sport when it comes to TV; two of the most eccentric racers these islands have ever produced and two men I'm lucky enough to call my friends.

My TV sparring partners genuinely intrigue people; in fact,

I'd say that the most popular questions I get asked are, in descending order:

1. *What is Eddie really like?*
   As wild in reality as he is on the TV.

2. *Can you get me a paddock pass?*
   Sadly, no.

3. *Where does Eddie get his shirts?*
   Do you really want to know?!

4. *I'm on holiday when it's the [add any race here] GP, can you sort me out?*
   See answer 2.

5. *Do EJ and DC really get on?*
   Sometimes.

6. *Can I have a ticket to the British Grand Prix?*
   I've already told you twice!

Much of my time outside of my job is spent standing in various supermarkets, on pavements or sitting on trains answering the same questions over and over, such is people's fascination with David Coulthard and particularly Eddie Jordan. Our show is a tricky balancing act, as we try to cover a very complex sport with the right mix of relaxed, honest banter and technical insight. Sometimes we get it right and sometimes we don't, but we're always well aware that, just as Lewis, Sebastian and Jenson are walking in legendary footsteps, so are we. Long before a former presenter of kids' TV and his pals somehow ended up on screen, a certain Murray Walker led the way.

Talk about setting the bar high! Murray, like many people in Britain, was bred on a diet of petrol fumes and race meetings. I recall spending the day with him at Brands Hatch in 2012; not long after we'd arrived he told me, 'I remember when this track was just a mud-and-grass oval in the 1940s. Back then, I raced motorbikes around here.' Murray admits he was never going to be a world-beater when it came to action on two wheels so in the late forties he picked up the commentator's microphone, something his father also did. From the Isle of Man TT, to his fiery relationship with the late James Hunt – in which Murray and James struck sparks off each other in the commentary box – he was simply *the* voice of motor racing in Britain. 'There's nothing wrong with his car, except that it's on fire!', 'I'll stop the start-watch!' and 'Go, Go, Go!' were the kinds of gems Murray became famous for – not perfect and not afraid to make the odd mistake, but neither was he afraid to put his heart and soul into his commentating, and when the big stuff happened he always got it right. In fact, my favourite example is probably when Damon Hill became world champion in 1996, and Murray said quite simply, 'And I need to stop now as I have a lump in my throat.' So much of broadcasting is about instinct and Murray's was usually spot on.

Murray is also unbelievably modest and I doubt he will ever realise just how much he's inspired people like me; quite often before we go on air I'll remind David and Eddie just how high we have to aim to match up to Murray, who has also been very generous with his praise. At Silverstone in 2009, when I was just a few races into my first season, he appeared at the door of our production office and, as a respectful hush descended, he looked towards me and then asked for 'a word outside'. 'Oh no,' I thought. 'Have I been so bad, and such a poor choice to lead F1 coverage for a racing-mad nation that Murray Walker is going to have a word?' In the event, he told me what a splendid job he thought I was doing, and how much he enjoyed the fun and the humour that we were managing to bring to the sport. I feel extremely privileged to have been able to get to know him – he really is a British institution – but I shudder to think that, on one occasion, I actually could have killed him . . .

Each year at Goodwood House they host something called the Festival of Speed, which attracts thousands of people. Part of the appeal is the famous hill climb, a race up the hill in which all manner of vehicles and drivers take part, from classic cars to modern F1 machines and world champions. It's a great day out. I was there with Murray in the summer of 2010, and was asked if I would drive him up the hill and give the crowds a chance to say hello. I didn't need to be asked twice!

They are very strict at Goodwood, and quite rightly health and safety is the number one priority. However, Murray and I were given special dispensation not to wear helmets as long as I kept the speed down. I was genuinely under the impression that the hill would be closed to all other cars until we'd finished our slow, show-off run, at which point the fast boys could carry on. So, in a queue of supercars, we eventually got to our slot, the announcer told the crowds that Murray was in the car and off I set. Wheelspins, doughnuts on the grass, generally messing around, I was giving the crowd a bit of a show. They were all waving, Murray was doing his best not to look scared by my slightly wild driving, and I couldn't believe I was sharing a car with the great man.

Suddenly, however, as I'm kicking up a dust storm on the grass and spinning us around, I became aware of a noise that sounded very much like a supercar at full pelt. Murray and I were just feet from the track around a blind bend, and as I looked over my shoulder, a modern supercar rocketed around the bend and up the hill.

Gulp. If we'd been on the track it could have been seriously nasty.

Instantly the thought popped into my head, 'You almost killed Murray Walker!' Now that is not the kind of headline the current Formula One presenter wants attached to him. I quickly put the car in drive, checked the road to see if it was clear and bolted up to the end of the course, quick as a flash and feeling awful. I tried to explain that Murray and I were a special case and were allowed to take our time, but as the owner of the supercar we almost mated with shouted, 'Are you crazy?!' at me, I quickly learned that no one, but no one, goes off-road, and that I'd just about managed to break every rule in the Goodwood book.

Thankfully, the man who has come to represent British success in Formula One with his distinctive voice and famous faux pas lived to tell the tale, the crowd of thousands didn't need to go home saying, 'I was there the day that . . .' and, funnily enough, Murray hasn't climbed back into a car with me since. How odd.

8

Driven to perfection

To put into perspective exactly what an achievement it is to sit on the starting grid of a Formula One race, think about the fact that on any given weekend in the Premier League 220 players will start the game for the twenty clubs that compete. In Formula One, only around 10 per cent of that number will contest the World Championship all season long. To claim a seat as a Formula One driver, you must possess raw talent, a mile-wide competitive streak, brains, brawn, guts, physical fitness and a huge dose of determination.

Formula One is known jokingly as the 'Piranha Club'; it's cut-throat, it's competitive and it doesn't suffer fools lightly. If this principle applies to the sport itself, it can equally be attributed to the fight to get into F1. From F2, GP3 and

WSR (World Series by Renault) to Euro F3 and GP2, there is a myriad of 'feeder series' that a young driver will take part in, in the hope of catching the eye of a team or a sponsor and getting the opportunity to compete at the very top. For every single young driver, from the 6-year-olds racing karts to the 20-somethings in GP2 (the rung below F1), the only aim is a Formula One seat. That is what everybody wants, yet so few actually achieve it.

Take, for example, a 13-year-old, who up until now has impressed friends, family and a few local businesses behind the wheel of a kart. Even racing at this age and level isn't cheap, and taking a step up the ladder also means taking a step up in funding. To persuade a team as big and successful as, say, McLaren to take a chance on you and provide that necessary financial backing to move up a series requires unbelievable skill and unshakable conviction. Many people have referred to Lewis Hamilton as an experiment in the design of the perfect racing driver. Formula One folklore has it that at the tender age of ten, Lewis marched up to McLaren boss Ron Dennis at an annual end-of-season motor racing bash and told him that he wanted one day to race for him. Less than three years after that supposed encounter took place in 1995, Lewis joined the McLaren Young Driver Support Programme.

Even when he'd been given the opportunity, though, he still had to reach out and take it for himself. Lewis's family had pretty much put their lives on hold at weekends to follow him up and down the country, spending hard-earned cash to keep his kart well serviced and stocked up with fuel, tyres and spares. Anthony Hamilton, his father, juggled multiple jobs just to pay for the family and keep Lewis's racing dream alive. Lewis had started karting in 1993, aged eight, and was soon winning in all the major categories at cadet level, becoming British champion along the way. And once the accolades started coming his way, so did that contract offer from Ron Dennis. The little boy from Stevenage of a few years earlier was growing into a fast young man, and McLaren wanted a piece of the action.

In 2001 Hamilton's racing career really began in the British Formula Renault Winter Series. He may have had his fair share of incidents and made some rookie mistakes, but he finished fifth overall, which led to a step up to a series called Formula Renault UK. The following season he became champion. It wasn't all plain sailing, of course. Towards the end of one season Lewis was given a two-race opportunity in British Formula Three. In the first race he suffered a puncture; in the second he had a collision and was taken to hospital. That didn't put him off, however, and late in 2004, aged almost twenty, Lewis got his first test for McLaren in an F1 car.

By now he was really getting noticed in Formula One and the investment McLaren had made in his career was about to pay off in a big way. For 2006 Lewis lined up in GP2, which is seen as the natural feeder series to F1; they share the same tracks and race on the same weekend. Lewis lined up along-side other youngsters who would eventually join him in F1, such as Nico Rosberg and Timo Glock, who still race Lewis today. In his debut GP2 year he pulled off some breathtaking overtakes, fought through the field when he needed to, and managed five race wins to take the title. McLaren had seen enough – it was time to cash in on their investment. In 2007 Lewis stepped into a full-time F1 seat, becoming the sport's youngest champion at the time just a season later.

What I love about Lewis is his visceral, instinctive way of driving. It's great seeing him up against Jenson Button because it's a weekly experiment in which two men in identical cars show how two very different styles can produce impressive results. Jenson really thinks about his driving, he studies the art, he makes calculated and smart decisions both in the heat of battle and when it comes to strategy, which is so important. He can also alter his driving style to protect the tyres or help an ailing car limp home. However, if he isn't happy with the car, Jenson can struggle. Lewis, on the other hand, seems to me to be altogether more emotional behind the wheel. He is driving in the moment, all his focus on that lap or that corner. In 2010, for instance, he crashed towards the end of the race in Monza because, although to finish fourth would mean a good haul of points looking at the season as a whole, at that moment catching Jenson Button in third was all that mattered to him. Then there was Valencia in 2012, when Pastor Maldonado was battling with Lewis for a podium position.

Perhaps, looking at the bigger picture, he might have let Pastor past, and focused on fourth being a great result in the championship battle, but not Lewis. He's a born racer, a fighter, he operates with his gut and his bravery, and at that moment all he wanted was to hold Maldonado off, which resulted in Lewis finishing the race in the barriers.

I think the starkest example I have personally witnessed that demonstrates the difference between Lewis' and Jenson's approach was at Silverstone, when I spent two consecutive days in 2009 driving with them. When I drove Jenson around, I was amazed by how nervy he seemed. For some reason, I expected him to have a relaxed attitude to health and safety – after all, he's not short on bravery. However, he gripped the passenger seat for dear life and shouted 'Brake!' at every corner. He then told me I was the worst driver he'd ever shared a car with, and that he was unnerved by not being the one controlling the car. Lewis couldn't have been more different. He almost came alive the more out of control or on the edge we were. When I drove Lewis around, it was a cold, misty day at Silverstone, just the kind of weather to make driving at speed more dangerous. Added to that, we were in a McLaren SLR, which cost hundreds of thousands of pounds . . .

I remember Lewis driving first, and he set off along the start–finish straight with the doors open! However, they were the gullwing doors that open towards the sky and as he floored it on the slippery track, the doors slammed shut and we whooped with joy. A couple of corners later he decided to see where the grip was, and as the back end twitched and he grappled with the wheel, he declared, 'There isn't any!' I love watching old footage of Ayrton fighting his car around the world's race tracks. One thing that always stands out for me is how much the car twitches, and moves around, looking for grip. Even in a straight line, on a damp track you'd see Ayrton extracting every possible bit of grip out of the track. And at that moment, sitting next to Lewis at the wheel, I got to experience the talent and effort it takes.

I must say, I was completely calm – after all, he does it for a living. However, eventually it was time to swap seats and then the fun really began. I was all over the place, as I didn't have the skill to keep the car fast and precise on such limited grip. But I had managed not to slide off the track, until I approached one of the corners and for some reason I completely lost control. As I was panicking about my off-roading experience, we were slewing across the grass; mud was splattered over the beautifully clean car and I was struggling to regain control, aware that once you've hit the grass, the barriers tend to come next. Amazingly, Lewis just giggled, 'I turned off the traction control, man!!' Very funny if you have his skill level and money; pretty scary if you have mine! We finished with him teaching me doughnuts by the pit wall, and when I asked if it was wise he replied: 'It's not my car, I don't mind.' Lewis is a very cool customer when he's doing what he loves, and has a great sense of humour that the wider world rarely gets to see.

He still seems to have the same approach he did the day he started racing in karts, which is admirable. He can drive at speed even if he's not comfortable with the car's set-up, but sometimes being quick isn't all it's about and I think he's understood that. To learn from your mistakes is perhaps the most important thing, and Lewis has seen his rivals challenge for the championship through consistency rather than race wins, and that is one of the biggest lessons he's learned. Patience – not always easy when you're battling for a race win at 200mph.

Lewis has had to do much of that learning in the F1 spotlight because he got there so early, but the path to F1 isn't always so straightforward. Fellow British driver Paul di Resta is similarly talented, determined and hard-working, but it has taken him a few years longer and a couple of sidesteps to get on to the grid with Hamilton. Paul is slightly younger than Lewis and, just like Lewis, he was a brilliant karter, lighting up the track and winning trophies when most young kids were playing football or getting into scrapes with their mates. In 2002, aged just sixteen, Paul got a chance to race in single-seater cars and started to show real promise. He was awarded a trophy as the best young British driver in 2004, but finding the money to fund his racing was a constant struggle. Thankfully, he caught the eye of Mercedes, and just when it looked as if he would have to give up on his dream entirely, Paul got the chance to drive in the German Touring Car series known as DTM. He really started to shine, regularly picking up race wins and fighting for the title, but still he wasn't where he wanted to be, which was driving in Formula One.

The world of motorsport is a very strange one, and for me one of the weakest elements of it is the feeder series. If you asked most people in the UK to name a player in the Football League Championship, one rung below the Premier League, I think they'd manage it; ask someone to name a driver in GP2, the motor racing equivalent, and they'd really struggle. It's as if Formula One is the World Cup, the Premier League and La Liga all rolled into one, the crème de la crème, where only a select group of drivers are able to compete. They are watched by millions every weekend, they are feted wherever they travel and they are true global sporting icons. By contrast, the reach and impact of the feeder series just one tier below hardly registers with people at all. GP2, GP3, F3, WSR – there are a multitude of 'feeder' series but I'd have trouble explaining to you how the pecking order is determined or even naming a handful of drivers who are competing. For this reason, a position in Formula One is even more coveted. A young, talented driver racing a car just a few seconds slower than an F1 car around a track might be within touching distance of realising their dream, inches away from becoming the next Sebastian Vettel; yet they race around circuits with few spectators, they walk down most streets in most countries without being recognised, and they almost without exception have to pay to drive. Quite frankly, it must feel like an entirely different world.

So when Lewis was winning races and the title in F1, Paul di Resta was impressing in DTM but was still very much under the radar. However, in 2011 he got his chance to step back into single-seater cars and he took the opportunity.

If a driver needs skill and determination to get into F1, staying there is quite another challenge. Take the example of a young German driver by the name of Nico Hulkenberg, who joined the Williams team in 2010 as he'd just entered his twenties. He came with a reputation for being fast, impressing in his rookie season and even taking a pole position in Brazil for a team who were by no means the quickest that season. Nico had seemingly done it all right up until that point – he'd won junior championships, worked at the Williams factory, waited for his chance and then taken it. However, at the end of that first season it was announced he was leaving the team, to be replaced by Pastor Maldonado. Many put this sudden departure down to the issue of money; Maldonado comes with incredible financial backing from his home country of Venezuela, and it's no secret that in Formula One money talks. Going racing is expensive and if a driver can bring both speed and cash to the table, then they become infinitely more appealing. Questions were raised about the motivation behind Williams's decision to replace Hulkenberg with Maldonado, with some suggesting that the Venezuelan was taken on more for the cash he could bring to the team than for the talent he could display behind the wheel. In Spain in 2012 he answered his doubters in the best possible way: he delivered the Williams team's first race win in four seasons.

It's always hard to know if a driver is with a team purely on merit, or if he is what people refer to as a 'pay driver'. For some people the idea of paying for the privilege of being part of one of the world's most high-profile sports is abhorrent; sport should be about talent and application, hard work and dedication, not money. It's an understandable point of view – I think if I heard that Manchester United were selecting a footballer who had paid for the chance to play, I too would struggle to reconcile myself with it. However, F1 is fundamentally different. With its high level of expenditure, money can genuinely make the difference between success and failure. Imagine a great driver is available, and so too is a very good driver. The very good driver is perhaps two-tenths of a second slower over a lap, but he also brings £30 million to the table each season because he has wonderful financial backing and his sponsors want a foothold in F1. That £30 million investment into the team's finances might increase the speed of the car by three-tenths of a second, which ultimately makes the very good driver a more attractive proposition than the great driver. Sport and business are always going to be difficult bedfellows, but that is the way the motorsport model works, because the costs involved are so astronomical.

It's important to remember that *every* driver on the F1 grid is an incredible talent, each of them having been granted an FIA Superlicence before being allowed to take to the F1 track.

I would imagine that in identical cars, the raw speed of all twenty-four F1 drivers would be pretty close, with tiny margins separating them and only driver talent making the difference. They all deserve great praise for making it to the very pinnacle of their sport. There are thousands of young men and women across the world right now who dream that one day they will get the chance to pull on a racing driver's overalls and call themselves an F1 driver. Unfortunately, karting requires thousands of pounds, single seaters tens or hundreds of thousands, and GP2 over a million pounds to compete in them. The huge investment needed to secure that prized F1 seat means that to pull on those overalls is also to accept the weight of a phenomenal amount of pressure, something an F1 driver has to contend with not only on the track, but off it too.

One of the things that really struck me when I first became involved in the world of Formula One is how huge a star a driver – every driver – becomes when he steps into the paddock. Perhaps it relates to the F1 bubble, but I actually think it's due to the fact that F1 is such a well-loved sport, a big global industry, and that those who follow it are incredibly loyal and committed – there are countless websites, fan forums, specialist papers and TV channels, many running 24/7 and all dedicated to what happens in the paddock. This intense focus creates a strange phenomenon: a driver might barely be recognised when walking down the street, but put him in the paddock and he can hardly move for reporters and photographers. Apart from the nine or ten really big stars, most of the F1 drivers could walk down Oxford Street and be recognised only by the hard-core fans. Odd, when there are just 24 drivers considered good enough to be in F1 – you'd imagine them being the 24 most famous drivers on the planet, but it doesn't seem to be the case for some reason. Some, such as Lewis Hamilton and Fernando Alonso, are global icons but would most people be able to identify a Charles Pic or Jean-Eric Vergne? Yet once they're in the paddock it's an entirely different story.

It might seem like an obvious observation to make, but when you're in the sport and winning races, you are king. And as soon as you're no longer at the cutting edge, there just isn't the same appetite for you. When I first started this job, Michael Schumacher was then a consultant at Ferrari. Still wearing the famous red, still at the races and still the man who had won seven world titles and who courted such controversy and success during his enviable career. I remember once walking into the paddock just behind him, and feeling a little nervous to be so near him – I had seen the fuss that surrounds the drivers when they are at work and I was expecting to be caught up in a scrum of epic proportions as he entered the F1 paddock. But there was none. A few people glanced over, one or two may have taken a photo, but that was all. I could scarcely believe it. Clearly, the fact that Michael was no longer in the car meant the need for a picture of him or a quote from him had disappeared overnight. It must have been very unsettling for someone used to being hounded day in and day out. Suffice it to say, now he's driving again he sprints through the paddock to avoid the madness and we can hardly get near him – he's like the Pied Piper of Hamelin, with the photographers' lenses constantly trained on him and journalists always on his tail.

Of course, the reverse can also happen, when a driver is plucked from obscurity and thrust into the limelight. Luca Badoer had enjoyed a pretty average F1 career, just a few seasons to his name, without scoring a point, and hadn't driven in F1 for ten years. However, when Felipe Massa crashed in Hungary in 2009, Ferrari needed someone quickly and Badoer was their chosen man. Suddenly, a driver who couldn't get arrested, he was so inconspicuous, was being followed everywhere by cameras and reporters, flashbulbs going off left, right and centre. I remember catching sight of a commotion in the pit lane and there he was, being asked his opinion on all matters Ferrari, suddenly at the epicentre of F1 and under intense scrutiny. I wonder how he must have felt. Getting the chance to replace an injured driver would be pressure enough, but then also to have to answer umpteen questions that could catch you out at any moment . . . it must have been really tricky.

Yet that is the bubble that F1 creates, the madness of a paddock in which the drivers are lauded and interrogated, celebrated and hounded in equal measure by the media. Luckily, our job as the BBC's F1 presenting team is very different from that of a print-media journalist in the paddock. Our aim is to make the sport as exciting and compelling as possible, and our focus is most definitely on the racing. In fact, we are almost the PR people the sport needs! Every race weekend we take a simple 90-minute piece of race footage, we trim it down to the very best 30 seconds, we edit it, put it to music and we turn drivers into rock stars. Effectively, we create a montage of their lives, with the sole aim of making them look great! We're not interested in their private lives or their business dealings; essentially, the greater we make them look, the higher we raise them on a pedestal, the more untouchable and talented they appear to the viewer, the more buzz the sport creates, which in turn helps to increase our audience figures. If the drivers look good, then the show looks good – a win-win situation.

Unfortunately, I do feel that scrutiny of the press is generally too great, which might sound odd coming from a journalist. I think a more relaxed environment would surely work better for everyone, and I often wish there was more trust between sports stars and the media. I guess the appetite for information is just too great, as is the desire to break a story, but one or two publications ruin it for the masses by putting their subject constantly on guard and prying into areas in which they have no business. The demands of the F1 calendar create enough of a pressurised environment as it is, without a driver having to face the added weight of media interrogation at every turn.

Lewis Hamilton is certainly less comfortable having to face scrutiny in the media on a weekly basis during the racing season, and when times have been hard he's been quite guarded and cautious, even with me. As far as I'm concerned, Lewis is the most gifted and exciting talent on the grid, but I think at times he is also a pretty misunderstood guy. It's always essential to consider context before you pass judgement and I think it's important to look at Lewis in the context of the life he has lived – always at karting races, always driven to beat the people around him, possibly unable to relate to the rest of the kids at school who weren't operating in a world of precision and perfection every weekend. Then you have the pressure from his dad to make sure the family effort and investment was rewarded, the pressure of being signed up by an F1 team at an early age, the pressure to perform in the cut-throat feeder series which can determine your future in the blink of an eye. That was all before he won title after title in the junior categories and was hailed as the next Ayrton Senna, at an age when most of us are still doing a paper round.

Lewis had a very different upbringing from many of his peers and even his fellow drivers. I think it is only now that he is starting to grow as a man, and it's tough for him that he has had to do it in the full glare of the world's media. I'm sure he'd agree that at times he's made mistakes, but I've been hugely impressed with the way he bounced back from arguably his toughest year in 2011. That season he had numerous scrapes with the FIA and we often joked that he had an 'express pass' to the officials so he didn't have to queue. Quite often the punishments were for unnecessary accidents on track, and the low point was probably the Monaco Grand Prix that year. He qualified tenth after being unable to set a hot lap in qualifying due to Sergio Perez's big accident as he exited the tunnel, which must have been terribly frustrating as Lewis knew he had a fast car. He then had a couple of run-ins with Felipe Massa early on, clashing at the famous hairpin before entering the tunnel at top speed side by side with Massa. By the time they emerged back into the light, Felipe had wiped the left side of the car off after smacking into the barriers, and Lewis received a drive-through penalty. Then, later in the race, Lewis clashed with Pastor Maldonado as they approached the first corner, Sainte Devote. At this stage Lewis seemed to be driving like a man who was seriously ticked off and, after making an overtake attempt late on, Maldonado ended up in the barriers and out of the race. Lewis received a 20-second penalty, and after the race he was critical of the stewards, making a reference to Ali G and the 'Is it coz I is black?' catchphrase that the character uses. Inevitably the interview was picked up by the world's media and Lewis came in for a backlash – something that he has learned to live with, but which I imagine never gets easier for him to deal with.

To my mind, what the 2011 season showed is that Lewis isn't just an incredibly talented racer, he is not just a proto-type of 'the perfect driver' – he wears his heart on his sleeve, and he cares passionately about achieving success in Formula

One. He seems to me like the driver on the grid least likely to accept the role of just 'making up the numbers'; he is there to win, and only to win, and for that reason he is enthralling. Of the current crop of drivers, probably only he and Fernando Alonso make me feel truly excited about what they might do during a race. That is not to say that I don't appreciate the brilliance of Jenson Button, the talent of Paul di Resta, or Mark Webber's incredible drive and determination. But when it comes to Lewis and Fernando there is an edginess and a brutality to their driving that to me sum up the essence of a Formula One driver.

David Coulthard and I were watching the cars pass through the notoriously difficult, high-speed Swimming Pool chicane in Monaco one year, and even DC was whooping with joy. The two men who really blew me away? Lewis and Fernando. Always fully committed, as most drivers are, but also both so precise, getting their wheels within an inch of the barrier every single time. Where other drivers were more hesitant on occasions, and perhaps an inch or so out of line sometimes, that was never the case with these two. They were metronomic. They were mesmerising.

Naturally, Lewis is also incredibly competitive. Now admittedly I don't do a job where my heart rate regularly reaches a peak of 190bpm, but I try to keep myself in good shape generally, so when I visited the McLaren HQ in Woking back in 2009 and there he was on hand to talk me through the gym equipment, I was ready to hold my own. 'How about we have a pull-up competition?' he asked. With hindsight, at this point I should have politely declined, retained my dignity and gone back to marvel at Ayrton Senna's title-winning car. But I didn't. No sooner had I taken Lewis up on his offer than he was on the bar, pulling himself up and down faster than I could blink. Oh dear. I was clearly playing a game of poker that I wouldn't win, and when Lewis eventually finished – not out of breath, not even sweating – it was my turn to step up. I gripped the bar, tensed my stomach muscles, took one last look at a rather confident Lewis Hamilton and tried to remember how many I'd need to do to beat him. Hmmmmmmpp. The camera crew busy filming us homed in on my straining face, as Lewis's confident smile grew to a huge grin. Needless to say, I failed to match him. Okay, let me be completely honest, I didn't even manage one pull-up, and Lewis has a wry smile on his face whenever he mentions it now, some three years later. Lewis is incredibly competitive, of course, but he's also incredibly fit.

I'm often asked whether drivers need to be physically fit to race in Formula One. When you think that an F1 car can go from 100mph and back to 0mph in under 6 seconds then, yes, they need rather strong muscles to deal with the ferocious car they're in charge of. Ross Brawn, the multi-talented, title-winning boss at Benetton, Ferrari and Brawn GP, credits Michael Schumacher with raising the bar of expectation and acceptability for Formula One drivers. Before Schumacher came on the scene, the drivers thought they were committed, hard-working and single-minded. Then along came Schumi, and he left them for dust. Nowadays the current crop of Formula One drivers are widely considered the greatest ever assembled and some of the fittest men on the planet to boot.

Few people have ever come close to the experience of racing a car at 220mph, just inches from a competitor. When it comes to football or cricket, we all know our limits – we've all kicked a football at school or in the park and been pretty rubbish, or tried an overarm bowl and sent the ball either five metres too high or five metres too wide, so we can therefore begin to understand the high level of natural ability Wayne Rooney or Stuart Broad must possess. The closest most people have been to F1 is watching a race on the television, and it's a sad fact that no matter what broadcasters try to do, the screen will always dampen the reality of Grand Prix racing. The cars are louder, the speeds are greater, the track steeper and narrower and the margin for error slimmer than anyone can imagine. It takes extraordinary physical and mental agility to handle an F1 car, not only at the fastest of speeds but in the tightest of confines – the car's cockpit.

To begin with, if your legs are too long or your feet too large, forget it. The smaller, shorter, more compact a driver is, the better it is for the team and the car's designer. Designing a successful car is all about balance and a smaller driver will allow the teams to move additional weight to other areas of the car to create perfect balance. If you are a tall driver, you are likely to weigh more, giving the engineers less leeway. For this reason a driver's weight is crucial, and the more pounds they can trim the better. Look at photos of racing drivers from fifty or sixty years ago, and you'll see a few of them were big men who clearly had no race-specific diet or training plan. Even ten or fifteen years ago the drivers were bigger than today and it was accepted. These days, if you are a tall driver in F1, as Jenson Button and Mark Webber are, you also have to be very thin but still amazingly strong – a tough balancing act. At the end of the 2009 season, when I was chatting to Mark Webber about how much he weighs, he lifted up his top and said, 'I know I need to lose a few pounds around here before next year.' I looked down and couldn't see an ounce of fat on him. A few races into the 2012 season I was told that Jenson's body fat was a staggering 6 per cent; I try to look after myself, and mine is 21 per cent!

The tall guys spend their time training, watching what they eat and looking pretty gaunt, while the jockey-like shorter guys definitely have an easier time. But once you're in the car and in the race, it doesn't matter how tall or short you are – it's going to be tough. You're on the grid, squeezed into a cockpit that has been made to measure for the driver, to the inch. It's tight. You're sitting on a race seat that has been shaped to the precise contours of your body. This is partly for comfort, because if there is an area on the seat that isn't perfect, over the course of a Grand Prix that discomfort will be magnified and could easily lead to a loss of concentration or even injury. But it's also for safety: another important aspect of the seat is that if you have a crash, its bespoke nature makes it as protective as possible. In fact, if a driver has a particularly big accident a light will turn on in the cockpit, and in that instance, the driver can, if required, be extracted while still in the seat.

Once in the car and on the grid, the driver has the task of staying as cool and calm as possible. During particularly stressful moments in a race or perhaps in an all-out hot lap in qualifying, the driver's heart rate can reach 210bpm, high enough to be fatal to a person not at the peak of physical fitness. That's a pretty significant hike from a typical resting heartbeat of around 45 bpm, which is the norm for the super-fit Formula One drivers. Next let's consider the added constriction of a driver's safety harness: with regular forces of 5g placed on a driver under heavy braking, and 4.5g of cornering forces, without the harnesses the drivers would shoot out of the cockpit. Such is the importance of being strapped in, therefore, that the belts are often so tight that the drivers can't take a full breath of air, merely adding to the physical demands on their bodies.

And that's not even factoring in the strain placed on a driver's neck when he makes one of those sudden stops or takes one of those fast, high-pressure corners, at which point the load exerted can reach a whopping 35kg. I recall once being driven around Silverstone by David Coulthard in a two-seater F1 car. Not only was it nothing like as powerful as a modern single-seater F1 car, but DC was only driving at about 70 per cent commitment. Even so, when he stood on the brakes I couldn't breathe; down the Hangar Straight it felt as though the helmet was going to be sucked clean off my head; and as we entered the corners I was convinced we were going to die. That day I was given a small button that I had to press and hold down. If I let go of it, a light on David's dashboard would come on and he would have to stop, because it would mean I had passed out. I kept the button depressed, managed two laps, and the following morning I couldn't lift my head off the pillow. Such is the brutality of a drive in an F1 car.

It's not only the driver's neck that needs to be strong; their upper body also needs to be in tip-top condition, particularly the forearms, shoulders and hands, because the effort involved in turning the wheel in an F1 car is just so great. As the speed increases, so does the effective weight of the car, so that it 'weighs' over a ton when at full pelt. A driver, who shall remain nameless, once told me that he had been given a dressing-down by his engineer for not turning his wheel quickly enough and so losing lap time through the Maggots and Becketts complex at Silverstone; the car was being pushed to the left, then the right, then back to the left again so ferociously that, despite working out almost every day, he simply couldn't turn the wheel back the other way fast enough. Martin Brundle also described how, by the end of one Monaco Grand Prix, the palm of his hand was bleeding because of the number of gear changes he'd had to make. In Martin's day the gears were operated by a traditional stick shift, whereas these days the drivers just flick a paddle on the back of the steering wheel – no small mercy when you consider that during the Monaco GP the drivers will change gear 4,000 times. So much goes on in the cockpit that we simply don't see, and all against the backdrop of the intense heat caused by the tyres, radiators, brakes and engine that are all around the driver. As a result the temperature in the cockpit can regularly reach up to 60°C, leading the drivers to lose up to two kilos of body weight and over a litre of fluid, and burn up to around 1,200 calories.

If the strain placed on the driver by the physical movement in the car is remorseless, then the mental rigours of handling the car are equally as unrelenting. Concentration is key for the full duration of a Grand Prix, which at times can be close to two hours. The drivers are constantly monitoring the way the car is handling, feeding back information to the pit wall that only they can garner, taking regular instructions from the pit wall about the way the race is shaping up, and making alterations to the car through the hundreds of settings accessible via the steering wheel. Certainly there are more physically demanding sports around; there are most definitely more mentally tough challenges than driving an F1 car; but there is simply no other sport on the planet that combines the physical and mental pressures of racing a Formula One car.

To be a Formula One racer takes more than just physical and mental fitness, though. We've all done a run on the treadmill and stumbled on dismounting the machine or bumped into someone as we've left the gym, too exhausted to look where we're going. Do that in a Formula One car and it might be the last thing you ever do. To drive a Formula One car, you need an innate calmness and you need nerves of steel. I remember in Hungary in 2010, old adversaries Michael Schumacher and Rubens Barrichello were running wheel-to-wheel on the track as they came down the start–finish straight. They used to share the team when they were at Ferrari and over the years it became apparent that one of Rubens's jobs was to support Michael winning the titles, which he did. However, in 2010 they were in different teams, and as Rubens approached the back of Michael's slower Mercedes, I think he could see some payback on the horizon. He had been getting closer and closer, lap after lap, until finally he had a chance to make the pass. Despite Rubens clearly being faster in his Williams, Michael was determined to save face and stay in front. As they slowly drew alongside each other, Schumacher started veering to the right. To the right was in fact the pit wall, but Rubens wasn't going to let some concrete get in the way of his big moment and he kept his foot in, missing the barrier by mere centimetres. Barrichello's actions are a great example of what is known in F1 circles as 'spare capacity' – in other words, some drivers are quick but the act of driving at speed takes up all their brainpower; others are slower but can absorb and process all the necessary information, such as the speed their rival is travelling, anticipating what the opposition is about to do or thinking about pit-stop strategy and race standings while battling for position on the track. The ones who are special have both speed and tactical nous, and the composure to employ them both in the heat of a race.

Interestingly, David Coulthard often claims that what was lacking for him was that spare capacity that would have made him a world champion. Sometimes he had amazing speed, other times he was able to read a race and make smart moves, but, he says, he wasn't able to do the two together often enough. I actually disagree; DC was and is an incredible talent, and you only have to look at how seamlessly he's adapted to television to see just how much spare capacity he does possess. When a TV show leaves me frazzled, DC has hardly broken sweat. And having spent the past few years on live television with David Coulthard I can vouch for the fact that F1 drivers just aren't like other people. DC's calmness and control in the face of pressure and surging adrenaline are most apparent when we are either in the middle of a particularly stressful and challenging show, or we've just ended one. I will turn to him and comment on how exciting or nerve-wracking the programme has been, and he'll just shrug as if to say his heart is barely beating faster, while mine practically explodes out of my chest! I struggled for some time to understand why this was, but I think I now know that it's all to do with our own individual thresholds. Some people might get a buzz from walking their dog and having a nice cup of tea, while I need live TV to get that same satisfaction, and David's bar is set even higher – he needs 200mph racing.

Driven to perfection

I remember sitting on the tyre wall on the outside of the La Source hairpin in Spa as David told me about the accident he caused there in 1998. He was hit by Michael Schumacher, a collision that took them both out of the race, and ironically allowed Eddie's cars to take a one–two finish – the first win for Jordan in 126 starts. It was a serious incident: Michael Schumacher had built up a substantial lead in the horribly wet conditions, and as he approached David's car to lap him, DC got the call on the team radio to let Schumacher through. However, David remained on the racing line, and with Michael unsighted by the rain he careered into the back of DC's car. David sat there, telling me the tale as if it was the most natural, normal thing in the world. I recall looking at him and trying to absorb the fact that this man had been at the centre of one of the biggest crashes of the 1998 season; he had been on the receiving end of a huge shunt by the most famous driver of all, and was then on the receiving end of that most famous driver's fury in the paddock after the race as Schumi sought him out with clenched fists. The crash and subsequent fallout sparked international headlines and caused shockwaves to reverberate around the globe. Yet here I am, sitting with this man over a decade later and in the very same spot, discussing it as pals, in the way we might talk about the lumpy custard we ate at lunch. It was a strange experience for someone like me, who will never feel that weight of a global audience watching and passing comment on my every move. For a top-level racing driver, it's just another day at their high-speed office.

Ultimately, that's what the track is for an F1 driver, a high-speed office where the drivers race for the progression of their career and the points on offer that day. On their shoulders rests the responsibility of keeping their sponsors, partners, teams and families happy, but what motivates them is the desire to beat their rivals. They are the most competitive group of people I've ever met, and they need to be given the quality of the opposition they face. At the start of the 2012 Formula One season there were a record six world champions on the grid; that's a quarter of the whole field, men who at one time or another have pushed themselves far enough to the limit, both mentally and physically, to win the world title.

It was Kimi Raikkonen's return to the sport in 2012, having retired in 2009, that boosted the number of world champions in the line-up to six. Kimi is famous for being pretty quiet and keeping himself to himself, but he's a real character. How many drivers would be eating an ice cream in the garage when the race might restart, even if he had retired, or retire from the Monaco GP and watch the rest of the action from a boat in the harbour? People often seem scared or unsure of 'characters' who aren't cut from the same bland cloth as everyone else, but sport would be a poorer place without people like Kimi. I was with him when he was introduced to Lotus Renault, his new team, on his return in 2012 and he was fantastic company, very cheeky and quick. It seemed he'd scaled the F1 mountain by becoming world champion in

2007 and then struggled for motivation thereafter. How great then that, after a break to recharge his batteries, he made his comeback and a couple of races later ended up on the podium following a stunning drive in Bahrain that left him feeling he should have won.

With a record-breaking line-up, we then proceeded to enjoy a record-breaking start to that season as six different men won the first six races, a statistic that shows how special the current crop of drivers really are. Without doubt, the playing field is incredibly even among these men, yet the winners are so diverse in character. You have Fernando Alonso – and there is certainly much more to Fernando than meets the eye. The most complete F1 driver for my money, along with Lewis Hamilton, I find him the most competitive and driven. He's also a bit of a dark horse when it comes to magic tricks – the chances are slim, but if you ever meet him and you want to make him smile, just ask him to perform one for you, he'd love it. One of my favourite personal F1 moments ever relates to Fernando: he was driving me around a track in a road car and I grabbed hold of the seat. I must have looked a little scared as I recall him giving me a wry grin and confidently saying, 'You are quite safe with me', before shutting his eyes around one of the corners and still driving it perfectly. Magic – and a great reminder of the skill level at which these guys operate.

Then there's Sebastian Vettel, who is mightily impressive. He can switch languages without even a pause and, in spite of all his success, is still very approachable and down-to-earth. I keep waiting for him to change, which is often the pitfall of becoming a global icon, but he doesn't seem to. He also has a great sense of humour. I was filming with him in China a few years ago, and we decided to do an interview while playing table tennis. There were a few questions being asked at the time about the legality of Red Bull's car, and rather than avoid the subject entirely he'd reference it after winning points off me by blaming his 'illegal aids'. Very cheeky but good fun – he shows an awareness of the world around him and an ability to embrace it, rather than be frightened of it. Of course, his grounded nature in no way reduces the competitive drive that he shares with the other top F1 drivers. Whereas usually a driver would just hit a few shots and then leave as soon as the filming was over, Seb and I carried on playing for a while afterwards. I think he was keen not simply to beat me, but to pummel me.

Sebastian isn't perfect, and like all drivers he slips up now and then, but he does seem generally only to make his mistakes in practice sessions. Any time someone questions his ability he does something to make them eat their words. Just as people were throwing doubt on his merit as a 'racer' – in other words, his ability to overtake and battle back if in the midfield rather than dominate from the front – towards the end of 2011 he pulled off some stunning overtakes and put his critics in their place. (He also pulled out some tasty dough-nuts on his team boss's lawn after the 2011 British Grand Prix. I guess it's one way to celebrate a win!)

Having come in for that criticism, it really was moving to witness Vettel's emotional reaction in Japan in 2011. As the youngest back-to-back F1 world champion, he joined an elite group of men who have won two world titles – men such as Jimmy Clark, Jackie Stewart, Ayrton Senna and Michael Schumacher. We had just interviewed Sebastian and I was told down my earpiece to thank Seb, let him leave and then wrap the show by throwing to the VT of previous double world champions. But, on instinct, I instead asked Seb to stay, and we played the tape to him, finishing the show by getting him to watch the piece of VT. As he started to well up at the realisation of what he had achieved, it was also the moment that I realised what a grounded and aware young man he is – most drivers are so focused on their own ambitions, striving for the goals they want to achieve, that it is rare to get them to embrace the bigger picture and put their achievements in context. However, as the music started to play, Sebastian's reaction was completely honest and human. He may have been surrounded by fans, photographers and TV cameras, but at that moment a tiny 7-inch monitor that we had hoisted above the crowd was his only focus. He stared at it, tears filling his eyes, and as it finished a huge smile spread across his face. He turned to me, his eyes glistening under the lights in the paddock, and said, 'What are you trying to do to me?' I didn't need to reply.

Since the end of the 2010 season, then, just how hard must it have been for Vettel's teammate Mark Webber? Of course, the rivalry that comes from constant comparison and assessment between teammates is all part of the fun of the sport, and is certainly nothing new – look at the great rivalries over the years, such as Mansell and Piquet, or Senna and Prost. Sometimes a driver needs that impetus and motivation from the opposite side of the garage, and I think that a bit of needle between team members adds to the drama for the viewers. In actual fact, considering that they battle each other at around 200mph, most of the drivers get on very well – they are at their happiest when in the car, racing their teammates.

Poor Webber was soundly beaten in 2011, race after race, as Seb romped home to his second title; it must have been disheartening, yet Mark remains to my mind the most grounded and level-headed of them all. He is one of my favourite F1 personalities and, far from being in the F1 bubble, he has a real connection to the world outside the sport, which I think is a really healthy thing. Politics, football, psychology, you can chat with him about the lot. His feet are as firmly on the ground as the day he started in the sport, and he has always retained an awareness of how mad the whole F1 circus really is. For example, the drivers have access to a mooring spot in the Monaco harbour, which they can use if they wish – some have a boat there; I believe others either rent the spot out or let someone else use it. As we boarded the plane to Nice for the race one year, I found myself standing next to Mark. We were talking about the harbour and as we walked down the gangway he delivered a great line about what he might do with his spot: 'If you ask me, mate, it's all showing off. I might keep the spot and moor up a dinghy – that would get a few glances.' I thought it was a great reaction, and if you ever see a dinghy moored up during a race it might just be his!

Webber is also a fierce competitor, however. After we went cycling once for a piece we were putting together about Mark's recovery from injury, we were chilling out back at his house and I noticed that he had lots of military pictures and memorabilia. I asked him why he enjoyed the two things, F1 and military memorabilia, and his answer was: 'Sport and war, mate, both the same . . . Just gotta keep fighting, keep going forwards.' And that is exactly the attitude he applies to his racing. In 2009 he broke his leg while mountain biking before the season had begun. He was hit by a car during a charity event, yet despite an operation, a nasty lump on his leg and a serious race against time to be fit, his commitment and determination meant it was never in doubt. It then emerged, as Mark fought for the championship in 2010, that he had a secret broken shoulder that he didn't even reveal to the team, but not even that could keep him out of the car – typical of an F1 fighter.

You don't have to be a world champion to be an F1 star, though. Felipe Massa, the most smiley and jovial of all the drivers, has yet to achieve the title, but he is a fantastic sports-man and extremely pleasant company. He clearly spends a lot of time searching to recapture the incredible speed that almost won him the 2008 title. Has he recovered – or more pertinently can he ever really recover – from the huge blow on the head he received in Hungary in 2009, which left a deep gash and a scar you can still see today? It's important to point out that the team, and his loyal race engineer Rob Smedley, say the accident hasn't affected him, so perhaps the fact that he's still chasing his first championship title is a stark example of how tough it can be to compete in the same team as the ever successful Fernando Alonso.

Paul di Resta is also one to watch on the grid. He, too, is yet to be crowned world champion, but he certainly has the time and the talent to make his mark, with one of the most down-to-earth and unfazed approaches to the mad world of F1 that I have ever seen. Paul comes from something of a racing dynasty: three times Indy 500 winner Dario Franchitti and sports car driver Marino Franchitti are his cousins. I, along with the rest of the sport, was impressed by Paul's arrival on the scene in 2011. Although he'd come from touring cars as opposed to a single-seater feeder series, he was right on the pace immediately. I remember sitting with him on the flight to the final race of his rookie season and asking him how it had been. 'Flown by, mate,' was the answer. 'How about physically?' I asked. 'Have you been drinking your bottle dry by mid-race?' 'Hardly take a sip, pal,' came his reply. 'How about your fitness levels generally, how've they been?' 'No problem at all, I don't know anyone stronger or fitter than me,' he said as he fixed me with a steely glare. The mark of a competitor indeed – a soundbite conversation that tells you an awful lot about why he is as fast as he is.

Of course a discussion about the talent in the current stable of F1 drivers wouldn't be complete without touching on the plight of Robert Kubica. Robert's accident just before the 2011 season was the first real example of the impact of Twitter on an F1 story. On that day I was hosting a football match for the BBC and gradually became aware that there was a story regarding Robert, because his name was trending on Twitter. Within minutes of the accident there were pictures of the damaged car, eyewitness accounts and reports of the crash. A video even appeared online of the next car in the rally approaching the crash scene. It transpired that Kubica had hit a crash barrier during a rally in Italy and it had pierced the car front to back, causing him serious injuries to one side of his body – terrible enough for anyone to recover from, let alone someone hoping to get back to racing in Formula One, which requires such feel and feedback through the hands. Just as we started to see reports about Robert's slow but successful recovery, he slipped on ice in early 2012 and reopened his leg fracture, which was an apparent setback. 'The greatest current F1 driver' was how Fernando Alonso described him recently. The sport is most definitely a poorer place without him, and I'd love him to return. It will be a tough climb back to top form but hopefully Kubica will be able to draw on those core strengths that separate F1 drivers from us normal people – a faith in his own physical and mental ability, a determination to improve, an unwillingness to accept imperfection and defeat, and ultimately an unquenchable desire to win.

And those are the traits I've witnessed so often since I first set foot in the paddock. The drivers will always be courteous, often friendly, but once the visor is down and the lights go out, they operate in a parallel universe to you and me. One where incredible speeds and eye-watering g-force are the norm, and where success is all that will ensure their place among the chosen few in one of the world's most competitive and cut-throat sports.

9

Savour the moment

Winning the Monaco Grand Prix is without doubt one of the greatest achievements of any racing driver's career. I've been lucky enough to spend plenty of time with David Coulthard, who won there on two occasions and often regales me with tales of just how tough it is to drive. I remember standing at the Swimming Pool chicane with him back in 2011 and we were right up against the barriers, which is a really rare opportunity in F1. Usually there are large run-off areas, then tyre barriers and fences, so to be a matter of inches away was a real treat. The cars were just so close to us, screaming past as their tyres fought against physics to keep the car and driver on the track and out of the barriers, and even the unflappable DC was caught up in the adrenaline rush of it all. He explained to me how at Monaco you must build up the speed over the days, slowly adding to your confidence as the weekend progresses to ensure that when it counts in qualifying and the race, you are really in your rhythm and have hit your stride. He revealed that the first time driving a racing lap there, back in the 1990s, he was initially unable to hold his foot to the floor all the way through the tunnel; it took a battle against every fibre of his body before he eventually managed it. His brain was in self-preservation mode, telling him not to do it, but he had the mental resolve to overcome this. Apparently, once he was so 'in the zone' when driving around the Monaco track that he actually felt as if he was driving through the barriers as opposed to up against them. I quizzed him on just what he meant by this and he said that, such was his proximity to the metal guardrails, he felt each time as if he was going to hit them but didn't. He knew at that point he'd nail a fast lap.

The circuit was once described by the Brazilian Nelson Piquet as like trying to drive a bicycle around your living room. He must have had a particularly large living room, but you get the idea nevertheless. And when a driver pulls back into the pits, it's a badge of honour to have scuffed the writing off the side wall of the tyre – that's how close you must be to achieve the honour of conquering the one race every driver wants to win. It takes precision, bravery and bags of talent, all of which Sebastian Vettel demonstrated in 2011. He was fighting off two world champions behind him in the shape of Fernando Alonso and Jenson Button, and as the race developed it started to look more and more as though Seb was going to be passed. His car was on older tyres than the men behind him, which would mean a loss of grip earlier and increased chances for Fernando or Jenson to snatch the lead. Sebastian had to be cool; he was looking to defend the championship – so becoming the youngest ever back-to-back champion – and a win at Monaco would do wonders for both his points tally and his mental strength. Six laps from the end, as his rivals closed in for the pass, a serious incident occurred behind him at the Swimming Pool chicane. The race was red-flagged for a short period, giving Sebastian enough breathing space to change to fresher tyres; he then defended for the final few laps before taking the win and extending his lead to a whopping fifty-eight points.

Imagine his delight as he crossed the line! He'd won the ultimate race of attrition, the Grand Prix where one mistake can end it all, and a race where the skill of a driver is put to the test more comprehensively than on any other circuit. A short while later, Sebastian has parked his car and, as is tradition, he's received the winner's trophy, then made his way on to the track to spray his team members with bubbly – the mechanics, engineers and analysts who helped carry him to glory. After that Seb was ferried off in a wave of jubilation and excitement to celebrate, as you should when you've just nailed Monaco.

David, Eddie and I headed out on to the track to film our live post-race show and I recall being hit by a realisation: we were standing on the start–finish line as we reflected on the race, and when I glanced down, there it was – the champagne that Sebastian had sprayed with such wild abandon just minutes before, drying on the track, slowly disappearing and evaporating into nothing. By the time we had finished our short filming, the champagne was gone, the moment passed, the road already being prepared to welcome back commuters, residents and race fans wanting to try out a lap of their own.

I am aware that it's the nature of the beast that things move on rapidly in sport, but it seems to do so particularly quickly in a sport as visceral and raw as Formula One. Each week there are joyous celebrations to mark the fact that winning a Grand Prix is an amazing feat, yet just moments later the success and the emotions attached to that success are forgotten. The sport, the teams, the drivers simply move on and those seminal moments that seemed so important just minutes before are consigned to history without a backwards glance. Gone if not forgotten.

I do think Formula One distinctly lacks the art of reflection, the ability to sit back and take in the wider picture while appreciating the past and making time to reminisce. There almost seems to be a fear that spending a moment looking backwards is a moment lost, a minute in which you could be looking to the future and moving forwards. Perhaps it's a natural consequence in a sport that is all about the next development, the next race and the next hurdle – the next victory.

A lot can be learned from Robert Kubica's single victory, at the Canadian Grand Prix in 2008. It was a great win for a breathtaking talent, and it put him right in with a shout for the World Championship. At that point in the season, BMW could – and some would say should – have made the call to really push for the final few races and try to win the title. To have designed a race-winning car is a significant accomplishment, and many felt they should have capitalised on the opportunity when they had it. However, it appears the team made the call that, having attained that season's goal of securing a race win, they would stop development on this car and focus on getting a head start on the 2009 model, in order to give them a good advantage over their rivals in that following season. How that decision must hurt with hindsight, knowing as we now do that the 2009 car wasn't particularly strong and that BMW ended up leaving the sport at the end of that season.

I did an interview with the team boss Mario Theissen live on the TV in 2009 and asked him if he regretted not pushing for the title in the previous season which, in retrospect, would have been the right decision. He looked at me for a moment, unimpressed, then pushed his chair back, said 'Thank you', and walked away. It was clearly still a painful subject.

How different would the reaction of the team and its driver have been if they'd known what was in store? A few years down the line, Robert hasn't won a race since and following his rallying accident it's uncertain if he will ever race in F1 again. The same goes for BMW – who knows if they will ever reappear in the sport? Focusing completely on the future was entirely understandable and in keeping with the prevailing attitude of F1 in general, but if they'd known then what they know now would they have dealt with the situation differently? I believe it's extremely important to celebrate your achievements as you make your way through your own individual journey; to be in the 'now' is a lesson everyone should learn.

I remember David Coulthard telling me that the driver is always the least excited member of a race team after a win because not only are their thresholds for exhilaration and joy a little higher than the average person, but they're also already thinking about the next Grand Prix, such is the pressure they put on themselves to deliver. I find that a little sad.

In sport, achieving success levels is such an intense experience that I imagine it's impossible, possibly even dangerous, for the sportsman or woman at the centre of it to envisage it ever ending. You focus on your triumphs, your belief in yourself is confirmed, and your desire not to let the bubble burst dissuades you from too much introspection. But the fact that life and sporting glory pass by in such a whirlwind makes savouring the moment all the more important.

Sport can be especially harsh: when your time is up, it usually happens quickly and definitively. There's no gradual winding down, and bowing out gracefully may prove difficult with the whole world watching. As a sports star you are as driven, determined and talented as ever before, but your own body begins to let you down – whether that's losing a fraction of your pace in a sprint, that split-second reflex on the tennis court or a swift mental decision on the football pitch. Eventually Mother Nature will gently remind you that you are not indestructible. There have been a number of high-profile cases in recent years of ex-professional sports stars struggling to come to terms with the tap being turned off, and I think that for anyone outside the sporting world the idea of retiring in your thirties is a pretty unsettling one. I imagine it's no less disconcerting if you're a sporting icon.

All our lives are transient, our successes quickly forgotten and our achievements eventually surpassed, but in few places is this so brutally exposed as in sport. After the accolades have been afforded and the plaudits enjoyed, the cosseted, safe structure that has been erected around a sportsperson often since a very young age is quickly dismantled, and suddenly they have to hope that the person underneath the talent and achievement is a strong, balanced, capable individual. The problem is that in many cases the real person hasn't had the opportunity, or the need, to develop and that is, in my opinion, why our sporting stars tend to struggle when they leave the stage. Some, like Michael Schumacher, will return to the limelight; for others it seems retirement is too much to cope with. History is littered with tales of men and women who excelled in the sporting arena but found that everyday life proved a far tougher challenge.

My experience of Formula One has served only to confirm my feelings on this subject. I have always used the phrase 'savour the moment' – I tweet it to my Twitter followers, remind my wife of it most days, and I've made sure I've taken my own advice since I started this job. For me, savouring the moment can simply involve standing in the pit lane and reminding myself how lucky I am. I vividly recollect being in the paddock of the Abu Dhabi Grand Prix in 2010; the sun was setting into a blazing red flare across the sky and one of four potential champions was about to be crowned at the end of the most dramatic season I've ever known. With the cars assembled on the grid and the whole paddock gathered around TV screens for the race start, I walked out into the middle of the paddock with no one else around. As I looked down at the ground a solitary beetle was scurrying past me and I have no idea why, but I followed that beetle's progress for a good 3 minutes as he made his way around the paddock. The eyes of the world were trained on this massive, most opulent circuit, and the dreams of the drivers would be realised or abandoned on this track, yet here was this beetle, and he didn't give a damn. I had been so stressed about whether I was doing a good job, so focused on how to deliver the best programme for the viewers, so caught up in the idea that the whole world rested on that F1 race, yet here was a wonderful reminder that, in fact, that wasn't the case at all. For a few minutes I just saw myself as that beetle, on this vast planet in our even bigger solar system, and it gave me a comfort that I think comes only from recognising that there are greater forces at work, and that whatever path your life takes it's important to retain that perspective. A multiple world champion, a high-ranking politician or a creator of wonderful music are all bound together by the one thing they have in common. They are just human beings, and what they do or their latest success may be of huge importance to them, but in the grand scheme of the planet and the world we live in, it's actually pretty insignificant.

One of the great things about the Grands Prix situated in rural locations, such as the Eifel mountains or the Ardennes forest, is that I'm reminded each time that nature will always hold the upper hand. Whatever we're doing and no matter how impressed we are with our own achievements, she wins hands down, and watching F1 cars race in the middle of the countryside is a great leveller for me.

At the end of that same race in Abu Dhabi, I witnessed another stark example of just how close the margin between success and failure can be. Fernando Alonso was the favourite for the title that weekend, Sebastian Vettel the rank outsider, and as we entered the final race of that 2010 season, Sebastian was fifteen points off the lead, a huge margin when you consider it would take him to finish third and Alonso not to score at all just for Vettel to end on the same points as the Spaniard. Ferrari, it seemed, were far more concerned with what Sebastian's teammate Mark Webber was doing in that race – perhaps as he was considered the greater threat, starting the Grand Prix only eight points behind Alonso.

As the race unfolded, Webber needed to pit after just eleven laps and Ferrari matched his strategy by bringing Fernando into the pits just a few laps later. Nobody could predict at that point whether an early stop was the right move, but it very quickly became clear that perhaps it wasn't. Fernando and Mark emerged from the pits into a congested midfield and soon caught up with the Renault of Vitaly Petrov; it must have been a hugely frustrating experience for both drivers, as they were desperate to overtake and fight for the title. But, at a circuit where overtaking is notoriously difficult, they simply couldn't shift Petrov out of the way and race up towards the front. The strategy had backfired.

Eddie Jordan, who was sitting with me, grabbed my leg and wailed, 'It's slipping away from Ferrari!' I wasn't sure if he was rejoicing or despairing, but he was certainly right. As the Ferrari race engineers urged Fernando on, the championship leader and Mark Webber in the Red Bull would have been well aware that they were losing the title battle. Meanwhile, Sebastian Vettel led throughout and no one was able to challenge him. He took the fifth win of his season, the championship lead for the very first time that season, and snatched the title away from the two men who were in the box seat going into the weekend. Seb had driven the perfect race, won in style and, against all the odds, he'd lifted the World Championship with three wins from the final four races of the year.

That was the remarkable thing about Sebastian taking the 2010 title: in the end, it wasn't a case of the better driver, faster car or stronger team over the season – one decision made in the heat of the race by Ferrari and Red Bull meant the first time Sebastian had led the championship, he was also crowned champion. Incredible. The finest of margins was all that separated the winners from the losers after an entire season of effort, sweat, investment and high expectations on the part of the Italian team and their passionate fans. The team had designed great cars, worked long days in testing, searched for the perfect set-up in practice, pushed the boundaries in qualifying and taken podiums and wins across an entire season. From team principals to the pit crew they couldn't have worked harder, and in the end it counted for nothing. In F1 it is victory or bust.

Back in the pit lane, the race now over, it was cold and dark in the Abu Dhabi desert. We'd finished our broadcast, T-shirts declaring Vettel as the champion had been handed out, champagne had been sprayed at seemingly every member of the team, and hundreds of news outlets and TV channels had carried the story of Seb's title triumph across the world. For a few short hours that circuit, those characters were at the centre of many people's lives, but now the madness had started to calm down. I quietly left the throng in the Red Bull garage and walked to the deserted pit wall. A bit like going into the garden during a party and looking in through the window at everyone enjoying themselves, I sat on my own under the night sky, taking the opportunity to reflect on how the rollercoaster season had turned out, and watched the Red Bull racing garage lit up with joy. It was ablaze with light and happiness, the music was pumping and the photographers were hoovering up any last snaps that might make the morning papers, while team members started the slow job of clearing down the garage with a smile and a champagne glow.

And as that scene unfolded I remember looking to my left and seeing the Ferrari garage, just a few feet away. They too would no doubt have arrived with high hopes of glory, probably packed some champagne, maybe even had T-shirts printed and glorious homecomings arranged. Yet now, this evening, here lay the dreams of the team in tatters. Instead of the music and the laughter, the Italian marque's garage was completely empty but for one man. A single Ferrari mechanic was standing in the corner, leaning up against the workbench, speaking into his phone. Perhaps he was sharing his version of events with the family, maybe he was telling his son not to cry, but I've no doubt that the hardest part of all was hearing the Red Bull music thumping away, hearing the laughter and the cheers that no doubt rubbed salt into some rather raw wounds.

That picture will always remind me of not only the emotional journey that sport takes us on, but also just how fine the margins will always be between winning and losing. A different decision in a pre-race meeting, a change of instinct on the pit wall, a crash by another driver – all of these things and more could have changed the outcome of the race. But they didn't, and a sport that prides itself on being precise, perfect and expecting the unexpected had been caught out.

It wasn't only the Ferrari team who had to deal with their emotions that afternoon. As much as drivers like to present a cool and controlled exterior, the reality is that beneath the layers of professionalism and steely determination, they share the same human emotions as the rest of us. I caught a fleeting glimpse of David Coulthard looking rather forlorn after Red Bull had clinched the title. Perhaps it was just that he was aware that the team he helped build had achieved the ultimate goal and it was all a little overwhelming for him. However, as much as he might deny it, I think he was also allowing himself a moment to reflect on how much it would have meant to him to be crowned F1 champion. It really was a fleeting glimpse, though – within 2 minutes he was back to his jovial self, and not a word was said about it.

When titles are won you get a sense of the high price of achievement. I remember heading towards Martin Whitmarsh to ask for an interview after McLaren had won in China in 2011; he was so overcome by the victory that, as I approached him, he dropped his headphones, he was shaking so badly. Or Mark Webber's unrestrained reaction on the team radio when he won his first ever Grand Prix in Germany in 2009. Team principal Christian Horner declared: 'Mark Webber, you are a Grand Prix winner!', as Mark whooped and repeated 'YES' over and over again before it sounded as though his emotions got the better of him. And who can blame him? At that moment the years of support, effort, determination and self-belief all come flooding back, and unlike many drivers Mark was forced to wait until he was in his thirties to taste what it was like to win an F1 race. In many ways, it was a snapshot of what it takes to be a success, as the teams and their employees spend their lives away from home, dedicated to a project that never lasts longer than a season and, no matter how much they give, people will always want more.

Yet despite all the sacrifice, we're all so eager to move on. It always amazes me that everyone leaves Singapore the day after the Grand Prix, when if you're quick you can grab the opportunity to drive around the circuit before they deconstruct it. Twenty-four hours earlier, the twenty-four best drivers in the world were battling for glory here, and now someone is taking those same racing lines in a Nissan Micra as they pop to the shops. Similarly, when we're able to present live on our BBC F1 Forum on the red button from the famous winner's podium, champagne barely dry on the ground, where moments before the world was watching, here we are on that same spot and no one gives it a second glance.

It's a consequence of the way Formula One works. It isn't possible for a football manager to update his squad on a daily basis, buying players every day and making sure that at each match the team is more talented than it was at the game before, but that is the core value of F1. The sport is a development race and as such there is no opportunity for sentiment, only for improvement. If you're standing still in F1, you can guarantee those around you will soon take the initiative.

I certainly don't think the drivers appreciate that their careers will pass by in the blink of an eye – they're too busy making sure that the career that does whizz by is a successful one. In 2012 two of the most experienced and well-loved drivers of the last decade were no longer on the grid, Jarno Trulli and Rubens Barrichello, who between them had raced in over 500 Grands Prix, celebrating more than seventy podiums along the way. They didn't have a seat to drive in the 2012 season, and as the teams arrived for race one, Jarno and Rubens hardly earned a second thought from most. At a football club, a legendary player will be invited back for match days or to host his own room. In F1, everyone is far too busy focusing on the future.

As always, the future revolves around finding the next big talent behind the wheel, and perhaps that's an even greater task given the recent success of Sebastian Vettel. In much the same way that Michael Schumacher raised the bar when he came on the scene in the nineties, perhaps Seb too has raised the level of expectation that teams have when scouting for raw talent nowadays. Can you win a race in the wet in an unfancied car? Can you take the title the very first time you have a car capable of it? Can you dominate your teammate and rivals, breaking records and being a double champion at just twenty-three years of age? No? Well, then, I'm afraid you might not be good enough. I just hope that there is someone whispering in the ears of Sebastian Vettel, Lewis Hamilton and their fellow drivers, reminding them of the importance of being in the now because as soon as the future arrives, the drivers are the past.

I guess I have the opportunity to savour the moment in a way that is simply not afforded to the drivers and their teams. For me, one of the greatest pleasures this job affords is getting a genuine insight into the emotions of a world-class athlete, to be so close that I can smell the sweat and sense the adrenaline surging through their systems. The final race is about the only time the atmosphere relaxes a little in the paddock, once the chequered flag has fallen for the last time, the remaining bottles of champagne have been sprayed and the season put to bed. I love the subtle change in the ambience at this time, and at the end of the 2011 season, I made sure I took full advantage of it.

Normally, as soon as a race is over, the cars are immediately under *parc fermé* conditions, which means no one apart from authorised team members and officials can touch them, as they're usually due to race again in a matter of days. In fact, not long ago we got told off pretty definitively on live television, just for venturing too close to the cars with our camera. The teams are normally at pains to stop idiots like me from clambering into the cars, because a broken F1 car isn't going to win a race, and just imagine if a badly placed foot or slightly too wide a bum ended up doing some serious damage. They're delicate things so it's easy to do, and in such a technical sport, if strict rules are not imposed and stuck to religiously you can soon run into problems. The cars are also usually carefully guarded in order to stop cameras and rivals from seeing what the teams have designed; it's often only when you get right up close that you can detect the subtle additions that can separate a winning car from a losing car. There's an element of pride involved as well, of course – these are the most advanced, most expensive racing cars on the planet. The sport is the pinnacle of motor racing, and to be the best of that elite group means you are on to something really special. The team are dealing with the tool that they simply can't do without, the one thing they must protect at all costs. Those cars really are the stars in this sport.

So, a couple of hours after the race in Brazil in 2011, in which Mark Webber had just claimed his first victory of the year, there sitting all alone in the *parc fermé* area was a Red Bull RB7. After an entire season of being wary and respectful around these cars, you can imagine my reaction when DC said, 'Hop into Seb's car, we'll take a photo.' I told him it was a ludicrous idea. Mind you, it did look tempting, sitting all alone . . . The 'race damage' that you don't see on television was quite apparent, with chips, rubber marks and various other battle scars all over the bodywork. It also had the most colourful wheels I'd ever seen on such a car – green and gold. You see, being the last race, and having already crowned the champion who was on the podium, the organisers fired a confetti cannon after the podium celebrations. Tin foil in the traditional colours of Brazil had filled the Interlagos sky, and then blown around and landed on the cars parked nearby. The rubber was still hot and sticky enough for the foil to stick to the wheels, and it had created quite an effect.

As I was admiring the tyres, DC reappeared with both a Red Bull mechanic and an official from the sport, who both agreed we could have a quick snap, as their work was done. I couldn't believe it! It was such a rare opportunity that I called over all the crew to stand around the car. So somewhere, on someone's camera, is a photo of me standing in the cockpit of the double-title-winning 2011 Red Bull, grinning like the Cheshire Cat, with the crew and David crowded around. A great moment at the end of a long and dramatic season, but also a scene that reflects the speed at which F1 moves on, how swiftly the mindset of its participants alters. If we had made the same request to any team in that pit lane just a week before, we would have been laughed out of town – or possibly thrown out of the paddock. Sit in our car? The thing we spend all weekend caring for as if it's our own child? The piece of machinery that can make our week or break our heart? No chance! Yet after that final race, that car – the winner of twelve races that season, one of the most dominant, successful cars ever designed – was obsolete. Last year's model. Out of date.

Once David, our kind friends and the crew had all walked off, I stood and stared at the car. Considering it was only a car, it was really rather moving. Having played its part and delivered every ounce of performance for the team over the past season, the poor racing car and the twenty-three others alongside it were suddenly expendable. Already the attention of the fans, the media and the mechanics was on the following season. What would the next car be like – better? Worse? Faster? More reliable? And what, just hours before, had been the greatest racing car in the world was now obsolete to the point that me and my clumpy size tens were allowed to get inside it. Ruthlessly, unemotionally, but completely necessarily, all focus was now on its replacement. And it's the way the sport will always be. How else can you go from racing around a few straw bales just sixty-three years ago to competing in cars that utilise some of the most advanced technology available in sport? From a sport that started in a disused airfield in England to a spectacle that is regularly watched by hundreds of millions of people across the globe, and turns the likes of Michael Schumacher and Lewis Hamilton into global icons?

It's hard to predict the future of a sport that has changed so much in sixty-odd years, but one thing is for sure: F1 must never become complacent about safety. I think it's only being honest and realistic to say that one day there will be another driver killed in the pursuit of speed; it's astonishing when you analyse some of the crashes, and consider the speeds involved, that we haven't lost a driver since Ayrton Senna in 1994. I don't agree with Stirling Moss when he says that F1 has now become 'too safe', although I know there is a fine line to draw. The powers-that-be need to keep making it as safe as they can, without blunting the spectacle or removing the challenge.

For example, the place where Sergio Perez crashed in Monaco in 2011 has since been drastically altered – the exit of the tunnel around the principality has always thrown up a challenge for the driver as it's downhill, a heavy braking zone and a sharp right-left. It's also about the only place in Monaco you can overtake, so it's an area of the track that encourages the drivers to take risks. After Sergio's crash, the barrier was moved back 14 metres, a change I approve of; the corner remains just as challenging, and you're still going to be punished if you make a mistake, but the penalty is likely to be a retirement rather than an injury. However, when shifting the barrier back, they lasered the road surface and found a sizable bump – a bump that had been there for many years – and so decided to resurface the tunnel exit. I don't think this was the right thing to do. As far as I'm concerned, an F1 driver should be good enough to deal with that bump, by either controlling the car if it becomes unstable or learning how to avoid the peril altogether. Having a heavy crash isn't part of the fun, but giving the drivers a track that really challenges them is. By my reckoning they solved the safety issue by moving the barrier, but by relaying the road surface they simply took away the challenge.

I think it's also very important that, while F1 embraces the future, it makes sure it doesn't sacrifice the classic tracks in a bid to explore its potential as an increasingly global sport. I understand the financial and political reasons for holding races in places such as Abu Dhabi or Singapore, and of course as the Middle East becomes a more important player on the world's stage, business shifts that way and so too does the sport. As ever, F1 and big business are intrinsically linked. However, if the classic races are left to fall by the wayside, I think the sport will become less of a draw for the new 'wannabe' venues. There is something that Silverstone, Spa and Monza offer that new tracks can never buy. It's not just the history, it's the soul – the memories, the stories and the comparisons of a bygone era. How can we monitor and measure the changes in the sport if we don't keep some of the legendary circuits? They allow us to compare directly with previous seasons a team and a driver's approach, tactics and, most importantly, lap time. What makes this sport so special isn't the name 'F1', it isn't the current drivers and teams and it's not even the speed – it's the heritage. Anyone, from a casual fan to a big-money sponsor, is buying into the legend of Formula One, a legend built on the likes of Jim Clark, Graham Hill, Sir Jackie Stewart and Michael Schumacher.

And what of the regulations and the racing they offer us? The designers will never stop looking to exploit the rules to the nth degree, their rivals will never stop questioning such designs, and it will forever be a compelling part of what makes this sport such a draw away from the track. There is more and more talk of closed-cockpit racing being 'inevitable'. But I'm not so sure. Isn't the fundamental of F1 that it is open-cockpit racing? I understand that it brings dangers, highlighted by tragedies such as the death of Henry Surtees, killed at Brands Hatch in July 2009 at the age of eighteen, when he was hit by a stray wheel that had been ripped from a car in front. Equally, the head injury Felipe Massa suffered in Hungary that same year, which could have been much, much worse, and the close shave Alonso had with Grosjean's car in Belgium in September 2012. I am happy for tyres to be difficult to heat up and even harder to preserve, because it takes smart driving, leads to exciting races and the drivers have to use tactics and take risky decisions, I like the push-to-pass button and always enjoy seeing the sport push the envelope – after all, the technology often filters down to uses in road cars, making everyday driving safer and more advanced. But I feel strongly that being open-cockpit defines F1 and should never change.

There are those who tell me that in fifty years we'll look back and not believe that people used up the world's resources driving around in circles before flying to the next track to do the same thing all over again. Like having a smoking area in a restaurant, or using a phone box to make a call, some have suggested that F1 will one day be prefaced by the words, 'Can you believe we used to . . . ?' I don't buy it. Man will forever continue his quest for speed, and if gas and batteries power him then so be it. The lure of going faster than your opponent, of risking it all to finish first, the thrill of a sport where a thousandth of a second can be the difference between victory and defeat – it will never leave us. I think we were born to race. Certainly Maurice Geoghegan was; many more since him have felt the same way, as will many still to come.

Endnote

In a book where the central theme is the speed at which F1 moves, it's rather apt that between writing the book and going to press, one of the biggest driver moves for many years came to pass: Lewis Hamilton has joined Mercedes. I first heard about it while driving along the M40 one afternoon, chatting to DC and EJ. The Italian Grand Prix was a few days away, and at this point no one had really mooted a serious Mercedes move for Lewis. As soon as I heard the rumour, I persuaded the guys that we needed to share it; I was determined that this wasn't a story we could sit on, so I made contact with Andrew Benson, who writes for the BBC F1 website. We agreed that it was an explosive story and one we'd love the BBC to break. It was a bold statement to say that Lewis was looking to leave the team he'd grown up with, but having discussed it further and made a few phone calls to check the sources, it seemed there was genuinely interest in Mercedes signing

Lewis. Time to let Eddie tell the world. That evening, I turned on the radio and listened to the news: 'According to former Formula One team boss Eddie Jordan, Lewis Hamilton may move teams and join Mercedes or 2013.' A smile crept across my face.

On reflection, it was as exciting as it was frustrating. We were informed by people very close to the Hamilton camp that 'anyone who reports that Lewis is joining Mercedes will be left with egg on their face', and that kind of statement really makes you question if you're doing the right thing, but you need to trust your sources, make sure you've done the due diligence, and also trust your instinct. When we arrived in Monza it seemed clear to me that McLaren were pretty annoyed that this news had become the talking point of the weekend. Our usually friendly relationship with their media team felt a little strained; in fact, Lewis walked right past us after the race as we waited to interview him about his victory – according to a member of his team, he was angry with us for breaking the story. That weekend, I left Monza certain that Lewis would leave McLaren. Three weeks later I was in the car, driving back to Norwich, when I heard the news that he had indeed completed the move. I was so proud of the BBC team at that moment: we had moved swiftly, believed in what we had discovered, and were the people to break the news to the world.

As for the move itself, well, perhaps understandably, some people said Lewis was only joining Mercedes for the money, but I'm of the opposite opinion. Of course, the financial aspect is always important but I think some fresh air, fresh faces and fresh challenges were far further up Lewis' ticklist. He'd been at the same team since he was a teenager, and in many ways leaving them was doing something we all must do eventually – fly the nest. He needed to prove he was his own man and make his own decision, and I think it may be the right one. Lewis also now has the chance to 'do a Schumacher' – when Michael joined Ferrari in 1996 they hadn't won the title since 1983, and he was able to build a team around him, inspire them and drive forward the technical side, turning the team's fortunes around and delivering what no one else had managed for over a decade. If Lewis delivers Mercedes a world title, it will be their first in half a century! I imagine it would also feel good to deliver success to a team when a certain seven-time world champion couldn't.

Lewis' departure might also prove to be a good move for McLaren too. Perhaps the relationship had run its course? Maybe it's inevitable that, over time, team and driver begin to take each other for granted. I think Sergio Perez will be fantastic for McLaren – he's always open and available to the media, he's brilliantly fast, young and driven.

Finally, what does it mean for Jenson Button? Well, he may well breathe a sigh of relief that he no longer has to share a team with a blisteringly fast driver. If he helps Sergio, teaches him what he knows and becomes the default 'team leader', it'll be great for the team. However, if he starts being beaten by a much younger man, it could make things tricky for him . . . As always in F1, it's about time. And time will tell.

Another big change since I started this book is that I too am leaving my job as presenter of Formula One for the BBC. I know my decision isn't a patch on Lewis' headline-grabbing move but, for me, it was equally tough. I had both job offers on the table in front of me, football for BT or F1 for the BBC, and one evening, with a Chinese takeaway, a bottle of wine and with Harriet's parents visiting us, I made the decision that I needed a change. There is no doubt that the opportunity to present live Premier League football appealed for a whole host of reasons: it's the greatest league in the world, it's our national sport and I've grown up watching and following football, just as I have F1. But a crucial part of the jigsaw puzzle was also having dinner with us that night – my unborn child! Harriet and I are expecting our first child, and that was a huge deciding factor. I imagined sitting in a chair at sixty years of age and looking back on what I was most proud of; without question, being a good dad and knowing my children properly won out over having seen the world and reported other people's incredible achievements. The furthest hosting the Premier League will take me away from my kids is Newcastle – a little closer than Melbourne and Kuala Lumpur!

In much the same way as Lewis had grown up at McLaren, I had been at the BBC since I was twenty years old. I too had grown up with them and I was probably more institutional-ised than I'd ever admit. I'd been given wonderful opportunities, had the chance to travel the world and fulfilled so many of my dreams when I became a BBC Sport presenter. However, when I first met with BT and heard what they had to say, I started to get incredibly excited about the opportu-nity of facing a new challenge. I felt that after four years on Formula One I'd given it my all; I had genuinely tried my best to change the face of how F1 was presented in the UK and I think we did a decent job. I love the idea of now trying to revolutionise football presentation. It's another great chal-lenge – not a comfy one, but an exciting one.

The actual ins and outs of how the BT deal was put together is a chapter for another book, but I would really like to say a huge thank you to you all for your support during my time on F1. From Harriet crying at the audience reaction when it was announced that I was the new presenter, to the wonderful comments online when I announced I was leaving . . . Quite a turnaround! I was lucky though; lucky to have a stunningly talented production team generating idea after idea, and an amazing editor in the shape of Mark Wilkin. Thanks too to Paul Smith, Niall Sloane, Roger Mosey, Philip Bernie, Barbara Slater and Ben Gallop for believing in me and trusting me to deliver a sport that British F1 fans are rightly protective and proud of. I'll never match Murray Walker, but I gave it my best shot.

I was also incredibly lucky to share the whole journey with

two fantastic mates. The audience nicknamed EJ, DC and me 'The Three Amigos', and I genuinely don't think I'll ever have that kind of on-screen relationship with any guys ever again. We enjoy each other's humour, know how to get the best out of each other and, most of all, we've genuinely enjoyed every single moment. Perhaps apart from the wing-walking above Silverstone! This is certainly not me shutting the door on the BBC or on Formula One. One day I'd love to return to both. Let's just wait and see what the future holds, shall we . . . ?

Acknowledgements

Wow, my first book and the fulfilment of a long-held ambition since I fell in love with the English language at Framingham Earl High School in the mid-nineties. I hope Mr Pugh doesn't spot too many errors! I'd like to thank my awesome wife Harriet, who dealt with me being away all the time – and when I was home, I was in the office writing this. To my great colleagues on the BBC F1 team, who didn't have a beer with me for almost a whole season, as I spent my time typing away in dodgy hotels. To my family, who have given me the two most important things a man can have – roots and wings. To Rhea, Jo and Jonny, without whom this book would never have got off the ground, Eddie and David for being the best on-screen brothers a man could wish for, and finally to you for managing to get this far – I hope you made the final chapter! I'll leave you with the motto that has served me well so far in life, I hope it does the same for you: 'Never sit in the comfy chair.' However, that doesn't apply when reading this book . . . I hope you enjoyed it!